TEACHING FOR FAITH

*A Guide for Teachers
of Adult Classes*

Richard Robert Osmer

Westminster/John Knox Press
Louisville, Kentucky

D0103709

Scripture quotations are from the New Revised Standard Version of the Bible, copyright © 1989 by the Division of Christian Education of the National Council of the Churches of Christ in the U.S.A., and are used by permission.

Book design by Gene Harris

First edition

This book is printed on acid-free paper that meets the American National Standards Institute Z39.48 standard. ∞

Published by Westminster/John Knox Press
Louisville, Kentucky

PRINTED IN THE UNITED STATES OF AMERICA

2   4   6   8   9   7   5   3   1

Library of Congress Cataloging-in-Publication Data

Osmer, Richard Robert, 1950–
    Teaching for faith : a guide for teachers of adult classes / Richard Robert Osmer. — 1st ed.
        p.   cm.
    Includes bibliographical references.
    ISBN 0-664-25217-6 (pbk. : alk. paper)

    1. Christian education of adults. I. Title
BV1488.075 1992
268′.434—dc20   92-9548

To Sara Little

teacher of teachers

in honor of her remarkable career

and enduring contribution

to the church's

teaching ministry

Contents

Preface

It is not possible for me to write a book on teaching without giving thanks to the many teachers who have influenced me at different points in my life: my parents, Dick and Skip Osmer; also Emmett Bringle, John Redhead, Louise Brooks, Bill Peck, Ruel Tyson, Bob Erickson, David Kelsey, Walt Lowe, and James Fowler. Although I did not have her as a teacher, Estelle McCarthy of the Presbyterian School of Christian Education taught me a great deal about teaching as we shared insights over lunch.

John Carr and Charles Gerkin of Candler School of Theology also must be singled out for special thanks. While a graduate student at Emory, I had the good fortune of working closely with John on the Pilgrimage Project, a research project funded by the Mary Louise Patton Foundation. Much of the thinking that takes shape in chapter 5 was formed through my work on that project. Charles Gerkin's thinking and writing on the relationship of narrative and parable informs the last two chapters. I am convinced he is correct to point out

9

the crucial role played by narrative in shaping human identity and the need for parabolic experiences that open up and reshape personal identity narratives in relationship to the Christian story. To both of these colleagues, I offer my heartfelt thanks.

In terms of the actual writing of this book, several persons deserve special thanks. My wife Sally has offered many perceptive comments along the way from her perspectives as minister and social worker. Freda Gardner, my colleague at Princeton Theological Seminary, and Joyce Walker, Director of Christian Education at Nassau Presbyterian Church in Princeton, read most of this manuscript and made extremely helpful comments. Outstanding teachers in their own right, Freda and Joyce offered many insights that enriched this book and helped it achieve greater clarity. Likewise, Walter Sutton, my editor at Westminster/John Knox, offered a wide range of help, from penetrating comments about the ideas in the book to help with the practicalities of layout and design. Mark Greiner helped significantly in putting together the Suggested Reading list. Kay Vogen, secretary of Princeton's School of Christian Education, has assisted in so many different ways that I cannot categorize them.

Last and most importantly, thanks is owed to Sara Little. It was Sara who sparked my interest in teaching, first through her own writing in this area and later as a colleague at Union Theological Seminary in Richmond, Virginia. Sara is one of those rare persons who combines competence and openness, integrity and humility, good humor and great seriousness. It is to her that this book is dedicated in honor of her lasting contribution as a woman, theologian, Christian educator, and, most important of all, as a teacher.

A few comments on the relation of *Teaching for Faith* to my previous work are in order. This book is an attempt to take seriously some of my own suggestions in *A Teachable Spirit: Recovering the Teaching Office in the Church.* There, I called for congregations to reclaim their theological task and become centers of practical theological reflection. The present book is an attempt to assist congregations in taking up this task. I hope teachers of the church will find it helpful to think theologically about the meaning of faith in ways that inform their actual teaching. In my view, this is the heart of practical theology: theological reflection that guides concrete action in the life of the church and its members.

Teaching for Faith also harks back to my first book in its understanding of the teaching ministry as a means of grace. This is important to point out, for it clarifies my understanding of the relationship between teaching and faith. This relationship is not a direct and immediate one. Teaching cannot "cause" faith. It is not like a dose of medicine that can be administered to a sick person and cause an illness to go away. The relationship between our teaching and the emergence and growth of faith in our students is less direct than this. Faith is a free gift from God. It comes into being in response to God's word of grace, made real and effective through the inner working of the Holy Spirit.

The teaching ministry, thus, cannot "cause" faith any more than any other human activity can. However, it can and does serve as a special human agency, which God uses to come to persons again and again. The basic assumption behind this book is that God has acted in a unique, unsurpassable way in Jesus Christ and that the church in its witness to Christ serves as a special instrument which God uses to bring faith to life. As John Calvin put it, writing here of the church, "For, although God's power is not bound to outward means, he has nonetheless bound us to this ordinary manner of teaching."[1] Building on this insight, Karl Barth once noted that God could use a dead dog to bring faith into being, if God so chose.[2] Ordinarily, however, God uses the church's teaching and preaching ministries to address persons, and humans are bound to these normal means of grace.

The purpose of our teaching in the church is to create a context in which faith can be awakened, supported, and challenged. Over the centuries, the teaching and preaching ministries have been compared to a farmer's planting of crops. The ground can be tilled, the seeds planted, and the crops tended, but in the end, many factors lie outside the farmer's control. So it is in our teaching.

On one level, this book is an attempt to help teachers better prepare the "soil" of their teaching. It offers many practical guidelines on how teachers can do such things as prepare good lectures and lead lively discussions. On a more important level, however, it is an attempt to help teachers reaffirm the importance of their work as a form of ministry. While teaching cannot cause faith, it is one of the important instruments that God uses to bring faith into being and help it grow. Is there a more important task in the church today?

RICHARD ROBERT OSMER

1

Why Do
Teachers Teach?

It is not unusual for those of us who are teachers in the church to experience two somewhat contradictory emotions. On the one hand, we feel called to teach. We realize that the church's long-term health depends on good teachers. Children need to learn the basics of the faith. Adolescents need to make the faith their own. Adults need to grow and renew their commitment to God over the course of their lives. We feel called to teach out of a recognition that the church will wither and die if it does not have a vital teaching ministry.

On the other hand, many of us have felt a different set of emotions at times. In spite of a strong sense of the importance of teaching, we have felt inadequate to the task. Few of us who are teachers in the church began our teaching with much experience. We are lawyers, business men and women, doctors, homemakers, and farmers. Most of us who teach spend our time doing something else during the week and have not developed the kind of confidence in our teaching that we have in other areas of our lives. Many times even ministers do not have much experience teaching. They may have taken a general course on Christian education during seminary but have not been able to develop their teaching skills on a regular basis.

A lack of confidence in our teaching can lead to frustration. We want to teach competently, but we are frustrated because we do not know how to improve our teaching. This is unfortunate, because it does not have to be this way. Teachers are made, not born. It is rare for a person to be a "natural" as a teacher—about as rare as persons are "natural" baseball players or musicians. Occasionally, teachers emerge who are such good communicators or so creative that they seem to be great teachers without even trying. Most people, however, have to learn how to teach the hard way: by reading, reflecting, trying, failing, and trying again. Many different types of people can become good teachers, but they have to be willing to work at it over time.

Two things are needed if we are to become good teachers in the church. First, we need a clear idea of what we are trying to accomplish, a clear sense of the purpose of our teaching. What do we hope will happen as a result of our teaching? How do the goals of teaching in the church differ from those that guide teaching in a school or a business?

Second, we need to develop confidence in our ability to use a range of teaching methods. We need to develop an awareness of and skill in a variety of processes by which to achieve the purpose of our teaching. Is a lecture the best way to teach the material? Would a discussion format work better? What are some different ways of organizing a lecture or leading a discussion? Confidence in our teaching grows directly in proportion to our sense that we have skill in using a number of different teaching methods.

This book is designed to help teachers in the church develop a clear sense of the purpose of their teaching and to familiarize them with a range of processes by which they can achieve this purpose. As they more clearly understand the purpose and process of their teaching, they will feel a greater sense of satisfaction.

Just as importantly, it is also my hope that teachers will develop greater effectiveness in their teaching. There is no more important ministry in the life of the church than its teaching ministry. Without a vital teaching ministry, Christians will not be equipped to carry out their vocations in their everyday lives, nor will the church be able to mount an effective witness to the world. No longer can the church depend on schools, colleges, and the media to reinforce the values and beliefs it is trying to teach. More than ever, good teaching is needed in the church, and good teaching depends on good teachers.

Teaching for Faith: The Basic Purpose of Teaching in the Church

Teachers in the church should be clear about one thing: *the basic purpose of their teaching is to create a context in which faith can be awakened, supported, and challenged.* Their teaching is for faith.

What do we mean by faith? Faith is a relationship of trust in God whose loving-kindness and faithfulness have been shown in Jesus Christ. This is the heart and soul of Christianity. The core of the Bible is a story of God's faithfulness to creation and to humanity, a story that culminates in the life, death, and resurrection of Jesus Christ. It is God's faithfulness that brings Christian faith to life. God is trustworthy, and in faith, we recognize and accept this trust.

Faith is not something that is brought into being by human powers alone. We cannot "cause" another person to have faith by our teaching. Faith remains a gift. It comes into being as humans respond to God's gracious word in Jesus Christ and place their trust in the divine goodness.

There is an element of mystery about why some people respond in trust and others not, why some people grow in their faith and others stagnate. We cannot force our students to have faith, as much as we might like to. Rather, our task as teachers is to create a context in which this becomes a possibility. How does this take place? What sorts of teaching processes best serve this guiding purpose? The answer to these questions can be found by taking a closer look at the nature of faith.

The Many Sides of Faith

The theologian H. Richard Niebuhr once described faith as being like a cube.[1] It is a many-sided reality. It is not possible to see all sides of a cube at the same time. It may be possible to see the top and two of the sides, but the bottom and back sides remain out of view. So it is with faith. At any given time, one dimension of our relationship of trust in God can be described, but other aspects of this relationship need to be kept in mind.

In this book, we will focus on only four sides of the

faith cube. Each side represents an important aspect of a relationship of trust in God and should guide the processes we use in our teaching. These four sides of faith are

1. *beliefs* about God that serve as the basis of our trust
2. an ongoing, personal *relationship* with God that brings us into a relationship with other persons of faith
3. a *commitment* to God as trustworthy that shapes the way we invest our time and energy
4. an awareness of the *mystery* that surrounds God and places limits on our understanding and control of God.

Thinking of faith as being like a many-sided cube can help us in our teaching in two ways. First, it can help us become clearer about the relationship between the processes we use in our teaching and the larger purpose of our teaching. Second, it helps us see why it is important for us to use a range of different teaching methods.

There is an old adage that says we teach the way we were taught. We tend to use teaching methods that we have experienced ourselves, especially those we have experienced repeatedly. Most of us, for example, experienced a steady diet of lectures in high school or college. When we think of teaching, we almost automatically think of someone standing in front of a group and presenting information. Often, we make use of this teaching method even if we did not enjoy it as a student. We teach the way we were taught!

Such a practice, however, prevents us from forming a clear sense of the relationship between the teaching process we are using and the larger, guiding purpose of our teaching. As we shall see, the lecture is good for some educational goals, but not good for others. It does not provide much time for discussion and for personal exploration of the subject, for example. Likewise, discussion is good for some goals but not for others. It tends to take longer to cover information and gets side-tracked fairly easily. Some teaching methods are effective for some objectives and not for others.

It is important for teachers to develop a clear sense of why they are choosing a certain teaching method and how it relates to the larger purpose of their teaching. Thinking of faith as a many-sided cube can be helpful in linking the processes we choose in our teaching and the larger purpose of our teaching. Some teaching processes address certain sides of the faith cube better than others. When our goal is to help our students explore the mystery that is a part of faith, for example, using a teaching method that is designed to transmit a predetermined body of information is probably not wise. Purpose and process are not working together.

Teaching works best if there is a fit between the teaching methods we use and the purpose we are trying to achieve. It is not possible to address all sides of the faith cube at the same time and in the same way in our teaching. Throughout this book, we will explore different teaching processes that can be used to address different sides of the faith cube. Developing a clearer sense of the way purpose and process work together is an important first step in gaining confidence as teachers.

Niebuhr's image of faith also helps us see why it is important to use a range of different teaching methods. This is necessary if we are to address different sides of the faith cube over time.

Why is this important? Like any other relationship, a relationship of trust in God becomes distorted when it becomes one-dimensional. If only one dimension of a relationship becomes dominant, it pushes into the background other important things that make that relationship vital and healthy. A marriage, for example, becomes stale when a husband and wife spend most of their time together focusing on household tasks like cooking, cleaning, yard work, and paying the bills. Of course, these sorts of activities are a part of their shared life, but when they become the exclusive focus of their relationship, the marriage gradually suffers. The partners do not develop the capacity for deep sharing or spontaneity. They become too task-oriented.

Our relationship with God is similar. It too has many sides. Unless we are given the opportunity to develop more than one side of this relationship, it will become distorted, just as surely as a marriage or a friendship becomes distorted when it is one-dimensional. It is primarily for this reason that those of us who teach must learn to feel comfortable using a range of teaching methods. Over time, we must strive to address different sides of faith, sometimes helping our students examine their beliefs, other times helping them deepen their commitment to God. While we cannot address all sides of the faith cube in any given session, we can attempt to focus on more than one during the course of our teaching.

In the following chapter, we will explore four sides of the faith cube: faith as belief, faith as relationship, faith as commitment, and faith as mystery. In the remainder of the book, we will examine different teaching methods that illustrate how each of these dimensions of faith can be addressed. Right from the beginning, it must be emphasized that other sides of the faith cube remain out of view in this book. Faith also includes obedience, freedom, love of God, and service on behalf of God's kingdom, to name but a few. Everything of importance about faith has not been said in this book. Attention is given to only four dimensions of a many-sided reality. These four, however, are complex enough, and as the book unfolds, this complexity will become more and more apparent. For those of you who wish to improve your teaching, here at least is a place to begin.

2

Exploring
the Faith Cube

In this chapter, we will examine four sides of the faith cube. In a sense, this will provide an overview of the whole book. Yet something even more important is at stake. Those of us who are teachers will be asked to think theologically. Too often, people think of theology as something that academic specialists do in seminaries or universities. Although theology is carried out in those settings, often with the use of highly technical language, it would be unfortunate if this were our only understanding of theology.

In the first centuries of the church's life, theology was viewed as something each member of the church was called to do.[1] All persons were seen as called to reflect on the entirety of their lives in light of their relationship with God. Teachers have a special responsibility to reclaim this theological task. Only as they begin to reflect on their life and their work in light of their relationship with God will they be able to serve as leaders in this task.

In this chapter, we will explore the theological con-

cept "faith." Only after we have begun to clarify what is
meant by this concept can the practical ideas and strategies that follow be used in a theologically informed
manner. If the goal of teaching is to create a context in
which faith is awakened, supported, and challenged,
then the first step is to understand theologically what is
meant by faith.

Teaching for Belief

The importance of beliefs in the Christian life has been
both overrated and underrated in the church across the
centuries. It has been overrated by those who want to
reduce faith to belief. It has been underrated by those
who do not think it matters what people believe, leaving
each individual to decide this for himself or herself.

Those people who overrate the importance of belief
tend to think of faith as the activity of agreeing with
certain clearly defined ideas about God. Across the
centuries these ideas have varied. Sometimes they have
focused on the inerrancy of scripture; at other times,
they have focused on the idea that Christ's death is a
sacrifice to an angry God. At still other times, they have
focused on the infallibility of the pope. In each case,
faith has been viewed as agreeing with one particular
belief or set of beliefs about God.

There are two problems with this reduction of faith to
belief. First, it teaches us to place our trust in a human
set of beliefs rather than in the God these beliefs are
attempting to describe. Second, it tends to narrow the
scope of faith in our lives. Let us examine each of these
in turn.

Even in our everyday lives, it is not difficult to see the

difference between a description of something and the reality being described. Imagine that you have witnessed a terrible accident on the way home from work. You are one of the first people on the scene and must try to comfort one of the accident victims who is in great pain. In spite of much personal anxiety and a desire to run away, you stay with that person until the ambulance arrives and the accident victim is taken away. Upon reaching home, your roommate innocently asks you how your day was, and you immediately launch into a description of what happened on the way home. No matter how hard you try, however, your words cannot convey to your roommate what it was like to kneel next to a badly hurt person and try to offer some measure of comfort. Your description and the reality remain distinct.

This is an extreme example of something that we experience all the time in our everyday lives: the distinction between a particular reality and our attempts to describe that reality. Our verbal reports provide some insight but fall short of capturing what the reality is all about.

How much more is this the case in our attempts to describe the reality of God? Our beliefs about God can never fully capture and express the divine reality. They remain partial descriptions of God that must be clearly distinguished from the reality they are attempting to describe. When faith is viewed as agreeing with certain beliefs about God, the distinction between human description and the divine reality is lost. Faith becomes trusting the truth of certain human ideas rather than trusting in the God whom these ideas are attempting to describe.

2 - The second problem with a reduction of faith to belief

is the way it tends to narrow faith to one part of a person's life. So much emphasis is placed on holding "correct" ideas about God that other important dimensions of faith are left out of the picture. History provides example after example of individuals and groups who felt they were the protectors of orthodox faith but whose social commitments were an inadequate expression of a relationship of trust in God. How often has theological orthodoxy lived comfortably with religious persecution or slavery or sexism? Our beliefs about God are only one dimension of a broader relationship of trust in God. When faith is reduced to belief, it runs the risk of isolating our relationship with God from the rest of our lives.

living the faith

There are dangers, thus, in overrating the importance of the belief aspect of faith. Faith cannot be reduced to holding certain ideas about God. At the same time, however, there also are dangers in underrating this dimension of faith. Unfortunately, this is quite prevalent in the church today. Many Christians feel it does not really matter what people believe as long as they believe it with sincerity. This overlooks the importance that beliefs play in the life of faith. It does matter whether people believe in reincarnation or the future coming of God's kingdom, in a God who loves all persons or one who only cares for the members of a particular religious group.

Beliefs do matter. They are an important part of faith. Perhaps the best way of thinking about the importance of beliefs is to see the ways they function in a relationship. What we believe about a person has a great deal of influence over the way we relate to him or her. If we think a person is a gossip, then we are unlikely to share confidential information with that person. If we believe a person is a highly knowledgeable auto mechanic, then we are likely to trust that person's diagnosis of our car's peculiar noises. Our beliefs about people influence the way we relate to them.

The same thing is true of our relationship with God. Many people are deeply afraid of God because they were brought up believing God is like an "Eye in the Sky" who watches all they do, keeping track of every mistake they make. Others think of God as a kind of "Big Therapist" who empathetically accepts every sort of behavior without passing judgment of any sort. In both cases, beliefs make a difference. They lead persons to cower before an angry God and conform to God's earthly representatives. They lead persons to live self-indulgently because God is viewed as never making moral demands.

The ideas we hold about God are important. They influence the way we relate to God. This is why teaching must pay serious attention to the belief dimension of faith. We live in an era when beliefs of all sorts are readily available. People are just as likely to latch onto the beliefs of a movie star on a television talk show as to the central teachings of the church. Perhaps more than ever, this means that those of us who teach must provide people with the kind of information and knowledge they need to form beliefs that are grounded in the Bible and the Christian tradition.

If our goal is to create a context in which faith can be awakened, supported, and challenged, then our students must be given the chance to form beliefs that are consistent with God's trustworthiness. How does this take place? Most importantly, it takes place when we teach people the stories of the Bible and their account of God's faithful actions, culminating in the life, death, and resurrection of Jesus Christ. How do we know that God is trustworthy? The Bible narrates the story of a trustworthy God. Even when our immediate experience makes us feel that life is against us, we can still trust God on the basis of the witness of scripture.

In addition to the stories of scripture, it is also important that our students be given the opportunity to form their beliefs in dialogue with the historic teachings of the church. Over the centuries, the church has reflected on the meaning of scripture and provided doctrinal teachings that attempt to state clearly what the church believes. These teachings represent the cumulative wisdom of the church. A denomination's confessions, creeds, catechisms, or doctrinal standards serve as important secondary guides to the reading of scripture and offer summaries of its basic beliefs. Even if we or our students want to challenge this heritage, it is important that we first understand the tradition that is being challenged.

Teaching that takes the belief dimension of faith seriously, thus, includes handing on, explaining, and discussing a certain body of knowledge that is the foundation of our students' ideas about God. It is not easy to lecture about the Bible or some aspect of the Christian tradition in an effective and interesting way. Nor is it easy to lead a discussion that helps people learn something new rather than share long-held opinions. Yet it is precisely the ability to carry out tasks like these in our teaching that allows us to support and challenge the beliefs of our students. In the third chapter, we will explore how to organize a lecture, and in the fourth, how to lead a "focused discussion" designed to teach new information. These are not skills that most of us automatically possess. But they are ones we can acquire if we are willing to work at them over time.

Teaching for Relationship

Faith is a relationship. It is a relationship of trust in God whose loving-kindness and faithfulness have been shown in Jesus Christ. It is not enough to hold certain beliefs about God. Many people think God is loving and cares for the world. Faith goes further than this. It is a personal relationship in which people actually open their hearts and minds to this love, placing their trust in God to the extent their lives are transformed.

One of our goals as teachers in the church is to give people the opportunity to deepen their relationship of trust in God. Sometimes this means inviting them to open themselves to God's love for the first time. Chances are good that some people in our classes have little sense of a living relationship with God. Even long-time church members frequently have not been given the opportunity to develop the relational dimension of faith. God remains a remote, abstract idea, often tied in with a sense of moral duty. Faith goes beyond this. It is a living relationship of trust in God whose faithfulness has been revealed in Jesus Christ.

It is for this reason that our teaching in the church must go beyond the transmission of knowledge that helps people form beliefs about God. Knowledge of the Bible, Christian doctrine, and the church is crucial. But it is not enough. This knowledge must become part of a living relationship with God. Sometimes the relational dimension of faith is called spirituality; other times,

piety. In either case, it refers to a sense of God's active
presence in a person's life and in the world.

Teaching in the church must strive to support and
nurture this relational dimension. Without it, faith can
easily become little more than a cold set of beliefs or a
zealous pursuit of moral obligations. It is only a living
relationship of trust in God that saves us from these
kinds of dogmatic or moralistic tendencies. If we would
teach for faith in the church, then we cannot avoid
focusing on the personal piety of our students.

How can we nurture the relational dimension of faith
in our teaching? The key to this, I believe, is the active
participation and sharing of the members of our class.[2]
To put the matter quite simply, our relationship with
God is supported and nurtured in and through our
relationships with other Christians. In recent years, the
"electronic church"—religious programs on television
and radio—has created the impression that people can
form a vital relationship with God in the safe confines of
their own living room. All that is required is to tune in
the televangelist and occasionally make a financial contribution to his or her ministry. This is a distorted
understanding of faith.

Throughout scripture, a vital relationship with God
goes hand in hand with an active sharing in the lives of
other believers. It is not possible for us to be Christians
by ourselves. Other Christians possess gifts and insights
we do not have. They can help us see the limitations of
our understanding of God and can challenge us to grow.
They can support us when we are hurting and need the
comfort of trusted friends. All of us need the active
support of other Christians if our relationship with God
is to grow.

One of the most important tasks we have as teachers is to build a sense of community in our class that allows our students to share with one another in ways that deepen their relationship with God. Admittedly, some classes gather primarily to learn new information and only seem to be comfortable with a lecture format that leaves room for little student participation. Such classes would resist the kind of sharing that is being advocated here.

There is legitimate place for lecture-oriented classes in the church. Leaders of such classes, however, would do well to ask themselves the following question: Where are my students receiving support for a deeper relationship with God, if not in this class? Perhaps there are opportunities for spiritual growth in other parts of the church's life. If so, fine. Many times, however, discomfort with class sharing is a sign that the members do not really want to grow in their relationship with God. They are more comfortable as passive receivers of knowledge than as active contributors to a supportive, challenging community of faith.

If our goal is to teach for faith, we cannot be satisfied with this stance. We must learn how to teach in ways that help our students support and challenge one another in their relationship with God. While this is not always easy, it can be one of the more exciting and rewarding aspects of our teaching. Moreover, it is possible for teachers to develop greater skill in facilitating sharing.

The heart of teaching that encourages student sharing is learning how to lead a discussion. The heart of leading a discussion, moreover, is learning how to ask good questions. Chapter 4 explores ways of becoming a better discussion leader and question-asker. The premise throughout that chapter is relatively simple: If people are to grow in their relationship with God, then they need to participate in supportive, challenging relation-ships with other Christians. To that end, we as teachers must learn how to teach for relationship.

Teaching for Commitment

A third side of the faith cube focuses on commitment. Almost instinctively we realize how important this di-mension of faith is. Without an abiding faith commit-ment in our students, it is difficult to get them to put the time and energy into deepening their beliefs or personal spirituality. Struggling to acquire new understandings of God is not easy. It takes a willingness to study, to rethink ideas that have been held for some time, to listen to others, and to act on new beliefs. Engaging in this kind of process takes commitment.

Defining commitment is hard to do. We know it when we see it, but it is not easy to put into a neat and tidy definition. Words like dedication, investment, and de-votion come to mind when we think of commitment. What they all point to is a deep and abiding care for something. Commitment to a sport, marriage, or job implies a high degree of investment, to the point that it shapes the way persons spend their time and energy. When we say a person is committed to playing tennis, for example, we have in mind the level of dedication he or she has to that sport: a willingness to pay for lessons, to locate a place to play, to find time to practice, and to play on a regular basis. Similarly, we might speak of a highly committed bridge player or a deeply committed student.

In short, commitment has to do with the level of investment that a person has in something. In the realm of faith, it points to the kind of dedication and devotion a person has in his or her relationship with God. National surveys show time and time again that many people believe in God and hold a variety of Christian beliefs but do not participate in organized religion.[3] It is fair to ask about the level of their commitment. Is it enough to believe in God and never go to church or make financial obligations on its behalf? What kind of commitment is that?

The same type of questions, of course, can be asked of those people who go to church on a regular basis. Is it enough for us to show up for worship on Sunday morning without participating in other church activities that can help us grow in our faith over the course of our lives? Is it enough to confine our faith to Sunday without relating it to the rest of our lives? Lying behind these questions is the issue of commitment: our dedication and devotion to the God whose loving-kindness has been shown in Jesus Christ.

As teachers in the church, we cannot afford to by-pass this dimension of faith in our students. This is why it is important to ask: Where does commitment come from? How can I provide opportunities for my students to deepen their commitment to God? In my view, the answers to these questions require those of us who teach to rethink the place of commitment in faith. We must move away from thinking about commitment primarily as a matter of the will and begin seeing it as grounded in the personal identity narratives of our students. In the fifth chapter, I will describe what this means more fully, but something of what I have in mind can be pointed to briefly.

Quite often, commitment is portrayed like this: Human beings are seen as having an inner self or agency called the will by which they direct their actions and make decisions. In this view, it is through the exercise of the will that people make commitments, including a commitment to God. They can choose how dedicated they are going to be in their relationship to God. Their level of investment and devotion can be high or it can be low. The choice is up to them. It is a matter of the will.

When this understanding is present, teaching commitment is seen as a matter of appealing to human will. Teachers are supposed to exhort, demand, and persuade their students to exercise their wills and increase their commitment to God or make a commitment for the first time. Sometimes, teachers even go so far as to put pressure on their students, hoping they can force a deeper level of commitment that way.

The problem with this approach to teaching is that it rests on a partial and, potentially, distorted view of the way commitment comes into being and grows in the life of faith. *Commitment is not, first and foremost, a matter of individual will.* We must rethink its place in the life of faith if our teaching is going to address this dimension effectively. Perhaps no theologian has seen this more clearly than the Protestant Reformer, Martin Luther. In his great theological treatise, "Bondage of the Will," he points out that the Bible portrays humans as captive to sin.[4] Every part of the human psyche is distorted by this reality, including the will.

Of course, persons exercise their wills to make decisions. We see this every day. People are free to choose whether they order this food for lunch or that. They can decide whether to get up when the alarm clock rings in the morning or stay in bed. As Luther pointed out, however, the fundamental direction of their wills is in bondage to sin. The many choices they make are tainted by self-interest or an anxious attempt to ground their identities in something other than God. The capacity to will remains, but it is badly distorted.

This recognition of the will's bondage to sin led Luther and the other great Reformers to place human commitment in a secondary position in their doctrines of salvation. In the primary position is God's work of reconciliation accomplished in the life, death, and resurrection of Jesus Christ. The commitment aspect of faith always is a response to this prior work of God on our behalf. We have our part, but it is a secondary one. Because of the bondage of our wills, salvation is a gift that creates the freedom to accept God's love and place our trust in God's faithfulness.

One way of seeing the secondary position of human commitment is through a comparison of humanity to a man who is in jail awaiting execution for his past crimes.[5] Right before the sentence is carried out, he is pardoned by the governor. The warden comes to his cell and shares the good news. The jailer unlocks the cell door. The pardoned man, sitting on a stool in the middle of the cell, is now free to leave. All he must do is get up and accept what has been done on his behalf.

Notice that everything of importance in this analogy has been done *for* the condemned man: the pardon, the communication of the good news, and the unlocking of the cell. He has a role, to be sure, but it is a limited one. He must accept what he had no power to do for himself. So it is with commitment in faith. Commitment primarily is a response to God's action on our behalf in Jesus

Christ, the acceptance of a pardon and a freedom we do not have the power to gain for ourselves.

Teachers must strive to place commitment in its proper place. Undue appeals to human will, creating the impression that people have the capacity to determine their own salvation, have no place in Christian teaching. When commitment in faith is seen primarily as a matter of willpower, positive thinking, or some other version of this view, the real basis of personal devotion and dedication to God are not taken into account.

Our task in teaching for commitment is a different one. It is the presentation of the story of God's love in Christ in such a compelling and meaningful manner that it begins to reshape the stories our students use to understand their lives. It is on this level, the level of what I will call personal identity narrative, that commitment is born and nurtured.

Only as our students begin to see the direction and purpose of their lives in a genuinely new way will their level of investment and dedication shift. Appeals to the will are not enough. Our teaching must undertake the more exciting and challenging task of helping students begin to reinterpret their personal identity narratives in light of the story of the trustworthy God found in scripture and Christian tradition. In the fifth chapter, we will explore how this can take place in our teaching.

Teaching for Mystery

The final side of the faith cube that we will examine is mystery. The Greek words from which *mystery* is derived mean "to keep silent" or "to remain hidden." We retain these meanings in English. A mystery is something that remains silent or hidden. It cannot be fully comprehended by human understanding. In mystery novels, for example, crucial parts of the story remain hidden until the very end, keeping the reader in suspense.

Mystery is an important dimension of faith. While the ultimate end of human existence no longer remains hidden, having been revealed in Jesus Christ, many things about God and the world remain mysteries. There are limits on what we can claim to know about God. In faith, we must accept these limits and not attempt to inflate our knowledge of God beyond the boundaries mystery imposes.

One way of grasping the role of mystery in faith is to see how it functions in ordinary human relationships. To a large extent, mystery is based on an acknowledgement of the "otherness" that is a part of every relationship. No matter how close we are to another person, that person remains an "other," someone who is never completely comprehended, someone who has dimensions that remain secret or hidden. It is not unusual to hear long-time friends say, "I didn't know you liked this sort of food" or "I never knew you played that sport while you were a child."

We see the same sort of thing on a profounder level in relationships of intimacy. For example, often, there comes a point in a marriage when a husband and wife realize they want different things out of their relationship. He desires physical intimacy; she wants emotional intimacy. He feels comfortable with distance in the relationship; she desires greater sharing. Each person comes to the relationship with different needs and a different style of communication. While each can work

hard at becoming more sensitive to his or her partner's
way of relating, a dimension of otherness remains.
There are real limits to each party's ability to understand fully the other person. An important part of any
relationship of intimacy is learning to accept this otherness. It is an acknowledgement of mystery.

This dimension of otherness is an important part of
our relationship with God. To be human is to be
"other" than God. We are a part of the created order;
God is the creator. We stand in need of redemption;
God is the redeemer. We are finite participants in
history; God is the sustainer of history. At the heart of
faith is a recognition of the otherness of God. God's
ways are not our ways. Much remains a mystery. As
Paul puts it: "For now we see in a mirror, dimly" (1 Cor.
13:12). An important dimension of our faith is an acknowledgement of this mystery.

One of the greatest temptations in the Christian life is
to try to press beyond the limits mystery sets for us. We
refuse to accept God as other. Across the centuries, for
example, many Christian sects have attempted to pre-
dict the end of the world. They have gathered together
and made special preparations for the last days. In so
doing, they have attempted to go beyond the limits
placed on what can be known of God: "It is not for you
to know the times or periods . . ." (Acts 1:7). Rather
than trusting God to act in God's good time, such
groups attempt to penetrate the divine mystery.

An acceptance of mystery in faith becomes especially
important when our immediate experience seems to run
contrary to what we know of God. Our faith tells us that
God loves and cares for the world, for instance, but we
see example after example of human suffering on televi-

sion. This becomes especially pressing when we experience this suffering firsthand—in the slow, lingering death of a loved one or in the sudden loss of a family member through a tragic accident.

Especially in such moments, faith encounters mystery. Our trust in God is not immediately and directly confirmed by our experience. We trust in spite of what we see and hear. We know that the mystery of God's will has been disclosed in Jesus Christ and that death and suffering are not the last word. Yet there are limitations placed on our ability to understand how this is worked out in our own lives and in the surrounding world. God remains "other." An important part of our trust in God must include an acknowledgement of this otherness.

It is for this reason that our teaching in the church must focus at times on the dimension of mystery in faith. There is a great deal of difference, however, between teaching about mystery and teaching for mystery. Our teaching goal is not to pass on a bit of conceptual information about the role of mystery in faith but to give persons the chance to personally acknowledge the mystery that lies at the heart of their relationship with God.

Teaching mystery brings us face to face once again with the limitations that are present in all teaching. At no point do we as teachers create faith or make it grow. Why some people come to faith and continue to grow in their faith while others do not remains a mystery. We dare not transgress the limits placed upon us by attempting to do more in our teaching than is appropriate. We cannot force persons to have faith or grow in faith any more than we can build a tower that reaches all the way to heaven.

What we can do is serve as an instrument in the
meeting of the Holy Spirit and the human spirit, the
Word of God and human words of confession. Accepting the limits of our teaching is a way of acknowledging
the mystery that is a part of faith. Our task, as a teacher
of faith, is simply to be "stewards of God's mysteries" (1
Cor. 4:1), as the apostle Paul once put it. We can do no
more, and we dare do no less.

3

Teaching for Belief:
Using the Lecture
to Transmit Knowledge

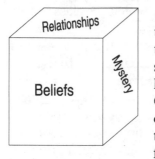

One of the saddest commentaries on the state of teaching in the church is the reality of widespread biblical and theological illiteracy. Whole generations of Christians are growing up without any knowledge of the central teachings of the church and their foundation in the Bible. While the transmission of knowledge is not the sole task of church teaching, it certainly is an important one. If we are to teach in a manner that supports the belief side of the faith cube, then we must make the transmission of knowledge an important priority.

Odd as it might seem, for much of this century Christian education has downplayed the importance of handing on biblical and doctrinal knowledge. In part, this has been a reaction against methods of education that used indoctrination to force people to learn the Bible or the catechism. Fear and guilt were often used to coerce people into accepting certain beliefs. Rote memorization took priority over understanding. These teaching approaches rightfully have been rejected by the church.

The importance of handing on basic biblical and doctrinal knowledge through teaching has been downplayed for another reason, however. This has to do with the dominance of an educational philosophy in Christian education for much of this century that places emphasis upon "experience-based" learning, an emphasis closely linked to liberal theology.[1] From this perspective, students are encouraged to "discover" the meaning of Christian faith in terms of their own experience. Teachers are not to focus on the *content* of what is being taught but on the *process* by which the class and its members construct meaningful knowledge. Typically, content is seen as less important than the processes of thinking and experiencing that students learn to use.

Recent research in cognitive psychology has called this way of thinking about education into serious question.[2] It is difficult to separate content and process as sharply as experience-based education does. According to recent research, people take in new information on the basis of the storehouse of knowledge they already possess.

Frequently, this storehouse is described as "background knowledge."[3] Every time we read a book or newspaper, we bring this background knowledge to bear on what we are reading. No author can state everything about a topic in a given article. He or she must assume we bring some information to the text. If the article is about something we know little of, then it becomes difficult to understand. In short, people process new data on the basis of the content they already possess. This also takes place in activities other than reading.

  When I watch a college basketball game with my two children, for example, my nine-year-old daughter has difficulty following the play-by-play commentary of the announcers, while my fourteen-year-old son frequently makes evaluative remarks about their comments. My daughter has almost no background knowledge to process the information she is receiving. She does not know what is meant by "traveling" or what a "run and jump" defense refers to. As a basketball player, however, my son already has acquired a sophisticated set of categories with which to watch and analyze a game. He not only can follow the commentators' descriptions of the game but also can evaluate their remarks. In other words, both children take in new information and process it on the basis of background knowledge they already possess.

  Cognitive psychologists describe the working of the mind by comparing it to information processing that is performed on a computer. Information processing is the activity of writing prose on or entering mathematical data into a computer. Three points of comparison frequently are made.

  First, before information processing can begin, the computer must be turned on. Similarly, the human mind must be "turned on" in the sense of paying attention to the new material. Unless we can capture and hold the attention of our students when offering them new information, there is little chance that anything significant will be retained.

  Second, once the computer is going, an existing file must be called up for new information to be typed in or modifications of the old file made. In the same way, the mind takes in and organizes new information in terms of the knowledge it already possesses. When listening to a person lecture on baptism, for example, we "call up" our knowledge of baptism and assimilate the new information into it. If we know nothing of baptism, then we must create a "new" file; that is, we must begin to build up information about baptism on the basis of what the speaker is saying. Cognitive psychologists call the basic units of information that are used to process new information "schemas" or "schemata." The richer and more complex our schemas about a given area of knowledge, the greater our ability to take in and understand new information about that area.

Third, a computer can only retain so much information in its memory before it overflows. Every so often, the information that has been typed in must be stored on a disk or a new file created. Moreover, until new information is saved on a disk, there is no permanent record of it. More than one writer has lost a morning's work when the electricity "blinked," and the file in the active memory of the computer was lost before it was stored. Similarly, we can take in a limited amount of new information in our short-term memory and must be given the opportunity to store it in our long-term memory. Only if new information becomes a part of our long-term memory can it be retrieved later and used to process new information.

If you are familiar with a computer, then this analogy probably makes good sense. If you are not, then it may not have been as helpful. And that is precisely the point! All of us take in and process new information on the basis of the background knowledge we already possess.

The human mind, of course, is more than a computer, and this analogy is limited. The mind has creative and reflective capacities that computers are never likely to possess. Nonetheless, the analogy is a helpful one in thinking about the importance of the knowledge we transmit in our teaching. We must take very seriously the biblical and theological knowledge we are helping our students build. Without this knowledge, they will not be able to read the Bible meaningfully. Nor will they have the schemas that allow them to interpret their lives and the surrounding world in theological terms. The basic information our students possess is important.

Learning how to teach new information is not an easy task. In this chapter, the focus primarily will be on the lecture as a means of transmitting information. This is just one of the uses of the lecture. Lectures can spark an inner dialogue in the hearers, bringing about a deeper commitment. They can move people emotionally. They can explore several sides of an issue, helping people come to terms with the limits of their own perspective. In short, lectures can do far more than transmit information. Our focus here, however, is on providing our students with knowledge that can help them build and strengthen their beliefs.

The lecture, of course, is not the only way this can be done. There are many other teaching processes that can be used to teach people new content and address the belief side of the faith cube. Many of these are described in books contained in the Suggested Reading.[4] In the next chapter attention will be given to the focused discussion, a teaching method also effective in the transmission of knowledge.

For many of us who teach, however, the lecture

remains one of the most important teaching methods. Our class may expect it or time constraints may make it necessary. In either case, we cannot escape lecturing, even if we want to.

The Lecture: Why Has It Survived?

Great lecturers are rare. Think back to your high school or college classes. How many great lecturers can you remember? If you are like me, you can count them on one hand. If good lecturing is so hard, why do teachers lecture so frequently?

One of the most important reasons has been mentioned already: "We teach the way we were taught." Having been exposed to a steady stream of lecturing throughout our high school or college years, we rely on the teaching method with which we are most familiar. There is another important reason why lecturing is used so often in the church. Sometimes the lecture can do what cannot be done as effectively through other teaching approaches. No other approach can communicate as much information to an audience as quickly as a lecture, while stimulating interest in the subject matter.

The staying power of the lecture over the centuries attests to its potential as a teaching tool. The lecture originated in the academies of ancient Greece. Book manuscripts were rare and accessible only to scholars supported by wealthy patrons. The lecture became the key way of handing on knowledge to large groups of people. Teachers would spend enormous amounts of time preparing their lectures, focusing not only on what they were to teach but also on how they were to deliver their teachings. Rhetoric, focusing on the art of public speaking, became the most important subject matter in classical education.

Lecturing also has been an important part of the church's life from the beginning. The early church instructed its new members through catechetical sermons.[5] Though sermons are not lectures, they are a form of teaching designed to hand on the basics of the Christian faith. During the Reformation, didactic preaching reemerged as an important source of instruction in the church, along with lectures given in the academies that the Reformers established.[6] At first glance, this seems odd, for the printing press had just been invented, making books available to the general public for the first time. Why did the lecture continue to be so important even with the advent of the printing press?

To put the matter simply, reading is no substitute for a good lecture. This is as true today as it was during the sixteenth century when the Reformation took place. Even though research has shown that reading allows people to absorb knowledge faster and with greater recall, it still lacks the face-to-face interaction with a talking, gesturing, responsive human being giving a lecture.[7] Good lecturers can help an audience discern which information is the most important and how to organize it for later recall. Accomplished speakers relate new information to the hearers' prior knowledge and respond to questions as the presentation unfolds. They can motivate students to learn more.

Good lecturing is difficult and requires a great deal of hard work and skill. There is no question that it is more difficult to use the lecture today than in the past. The advent of television, video tapes, and movies has made

today's students more visually oriented. They are used
to seeing things, not hearing them. They are used to
seeing things that shift rapidly from one scene to another. The result has been a reduction in the attention
span of children and adults, especially when it comes to
listening to others speak.[8] Some experts estimate the
attention span of the average adult listening to oral
communication is now ten minutes.

Thus, it is no wonder that lecturing is more difficult
today than in the past. This being the case, why should
we lecture at all? Why not use video resources geared to
the media-shaped consciousness of our students? The
answer to this is twofold.

First, while video tapes have a legitimate place in
teaching, they are quite expensive to produce and to
acquire. It is not possible, financially or conceptually, to
develop them for every subject that needs to be addressed in the church. Many churches cannot afford
these resources, even when they are available.

Second, there are many aspects of the Christian faith
that cannot be reduced to a highly simplified, media-
oriented format. Much knowledge important to the
Christian life is complex. Such knowledge is best acquired
in a gradual, cumulative fashion, under the guidance of a
teacher who can build on the background knowledge the
students already possess, dialogue with their questions,
and provide them with help in relating this new knowledge to their lives. The personal convictions of the
teacher, communicated in many different ways, also are
extremely important. Canned media presentations cannot do these things as well as a good lecture.

For these reasons, lecturing is an art that we, as
teachers, must strive to acquire. It never has been easy

to lecture well; however, we can improve our skills with this method, if we are willing to work at our lecturing over time.

Below are some ideas that might be helpful in planning and delivering lectures. These ideas emerge out of my own teaching and the teaching and research of others. They remain, however, suggestions. It is not possible to outline a foolproof, step-by-step approach to lecturing that will work for every teacher. Much depends on each teacher's gifts, skills, creativity, and background. Much also depends on the class: how it learns best and the teaching approach it is used to. What follows are some practical ideas that might prove helpful to individual teachers in discovering their own particular approach to preparing and delivering a lecture.

The Idea Outline

One of the first steps that many people find helpful when organizing a lecture is creating an idea outline. This may be done in the following manner.

We begin by investigating the subject matter we are going to cover. Most of the time this includes background reading: a book or denominational curriculum being studied by the class. Often, it is helpful to mark up the book while reading it to underscore the main points. Some people like to underline or highlight; others put checks in the margin; still others use parentheses to mark the beginning and end of an important idea. Marking the reading makes it easier for us to go back and pick out the important ideas. If this is not possible, jotting down brief notes is equally helpful, although it takes a bit longer.

Once this reading has been done, we are ready to form an idea outline. This is done by looking over what we marked in the book or jotted down in our notes and deciding on the points we are going to cover. It is not necessary to worry at this point about getting the ideas in order. We are simply trying to discern the most important ideas in the reading and the ones that we want to cover in class.

We create an idea outline by jotting down these ideas on a piece of paper with some space in between each idea. As we write down each idea, often, subpoints and examples come to us immediately. These can be written down under the main idea to which they are related. It is helpful to indent these subpoints and to leave room for thoughts that occur to us at a later point.

Our next task is to decide which of the ideas jotted down can actually be covered in our lecture. We have to be ruthlessly selective at this point and include only those ideas that can be covered realistically in one lecture. This is because people can take in and remember only a limited amount of information at any one time. As was pointed out earlier, our short-term memory is limited. Some research indicates people can take in three or four points at most in a fifty-minute period.[9] Trying to cram in too much information actually reduces the amount of learning that takes place. This is the time to remember the old adage, "Less is more." When our students' short-term memory has reached its capacity, adding more information is like continuing to pour water in a glass that is already full. It simply overflows and is not taken in.

In deciding how many points to include in our idea outline, it is helpful to consider time constraints. How

much time is available for the lecture? A full hour,
forty-five minutes, or only thirty minutes? Do people
wander in for the first ten minutes of class? Does half
the class leave early for choir? Do certain class members
always need time to give their opinion or ask questions?

There is no one right way of responding to these kinds
of issues. Some teachers, for example, believe in starting on time no matter what and like to go as long as the
class is scheduled to run in order to set basic standards
for the class. "Why penalize those people who get there
on time?" they reason. Other teachers adapt to the
class's natural rhythms and use the first part for socializ-
ing and the last part for questions, limiting their lecture
to the time when the whole class is actually gathered.
This eliminates interruptions and allows for focused
attention on the lecture.

In addition to time constraints, other factors often
enter into our decision about which ideas to keep and
which to let go. We might ask ourselves three additional
questions: Which ideas did our reading emphasize as the
most important ones? Which ideas do our students need
to deal with the most? Which ideas do we personally
care about the most and can lecture on with conviction?
There is no clear-cut rule for deciding which question
should take priority in a given lecture. Normally, some
sort of balance is best.

Once we have decided which ideas to eliminate, it
is often helpful to cross them out on our idea outline.
We now have the basic ideas we are going to cover
in our lecture. A second step many teachers find helpful
is the creation of a *presentation outline*. This serves as
the actual outline we will use in the delivery of our
lecture.

The Presentation Outline

Many times the idea outline we have created follows closely the reading we are drawing on for our lecture. The way we present the basic points of our lecture, however, *may not* parallel the flow of the reading done in preparation. Our task in every lecture is to present the material in a manner our students can understand; it is not merely to summarize the reading. If we are only going to summarize the reading, why not give our students the book? Our job in a lecture is to tailor the ideas we are presenting to our particular group of students.

Assessing Background Knowledge

In preparing a presentation outline, then, it is often helpful for us to begin by asking, "What do my students know about these ideas already?" As noted earlier, research indicates background knowledge is extremely important in determining how well people can grasp and store new information. For example, a group that has studied Paul's epistle to the Romans already has in place certain ideas that will enhance its ability to take in new information about his epistle to the Galatians. The group will have some idea what the theme of justification by grace means. It will have encountered Paul's understanding of the law and the Spirit. New information on Galatians can build on these ideas. In contrast, a group that knows very little about Paul's writings will have to be approached in a different way. A foundation of knowledge about Paul will have to be laid.

In trying to discern the background knowledge our students already possess, it may be helpful to ask two kinds of questions. First, what ideas do our students already have about the subject of the lecture? Second, what do they know about the lecture topic in their own life experience?

The first question focuses on the information our students already possess about the lecture subject. Using the example given above, what do they know about Paul or the Pauline teachings? Can we build on this knowledge? Do we need to correct distorted ideas? In new areas we may need to begin from scratch.

In the second question, we are going beyond information to a different kind of knowledge: firsthand experience of the focal topic of the lecture. A group may know very little of Paul's doctrine of justification, for example, but know a great deal about personal forgiveness. This may be all that can be presupposed in the lecture. Firsthand experience serves as an important connecting point between the new information in the lecture and the knowledge our students already possess.

The Organizing Principle

Once we have evaluated the background knowledge of our students, we are faced with a key decision in forming a presentation outline: <u>What overall principle are we going to use to organize our lecture</u>? Think of lecturing as similar to leading a group on a trip. How will the trip be organized? Is it a study tour, rigorously preplanned in order to visit as many places as possible? Or is it a leisurely jaunt with no reservations made in advance, allowing freedom to pursue those things that catch the group's fancy?

When we lecture, we are taking people on a kind of

trip. An important decision we must make is to choose
the principle by which the trip is organized. Often, this
is called the organizing principle.[10] Here are some common ways of organizing a lecture:

- begin with a problem, move toward its solution;
- state one side of an issue, then the opposite side,
  then present a possible resolution;
- set forth an idea, move toward its application in life;
- present events or ideas in their historical sequence:
  first this occurred, then that, and so on;
- begin with a familiar idea or experience, then examine it critically, making it unfamiliar.

There are many other ways lectures can be organized.
Choosing an organizing principle that can guide the
presentation of our ideas is an essential step. Remember, our goal is not simply to summarize the reading we
have done. It is to present ideas in a manner tailored to
the background and needs of the people we teach. If an
idea outline was created at an earlier point, we should
look back over it and consider several possible ways of
organizing the ideas for presentation. As a general rule,
lectures should begin with what students already know
and take them to a new destination. What sort of trip do
we want to plan?

Creating the Outline: The Introduction

Once we have decided on the organizing principle of
the lecture, we are ready to create the presentation
outline. Many teachers find it helpful to think of the
lecture as falling into four basic parts: the introduction,
the body, periodic summaries, and the conclusion.[11]

These four parts provide the basic structure of the presentation outline and are knit together on the basis of the organizing principle. In this section, we will examine the introduction.

A good introduction does at least two things: it gets our students' attention and sets in motion the flow of the lecture in accordance with our organizing principle. As has been noted, a key to handing on new knowledge is getting and keeping our students' attention. Research indicates that during a lecture the class's attention gradually increases for the first ten minutes and then begins to fall off.[12] This is one of the factors that makes lecturing such a difficult task.

To get our students' attention, it is a good idea to begin with a "grabber." This is an idea that stimulates curiosity, creates an expectation, or fosters tension. Just as a good mystery novel captures our attention almost immediately and keeps us reading till the end, a good lecture must "grab" the attention of the audience. Some people like to use humor. Others like to begin with a story or an example that relates the topic to the students' lives. Regardless of how the lecture begins, we should try to capture our students' attention and to focus it on the material we are going to present.

The introduction also tries to set in motion the basic flow of the lecture along the lines of the organizing principle. For example, if we have decided to organize the lecture in terms of a question-to-answer flow, our task in the introduction is to present the question the rest of the lecture is attempting to answer. In the same way, if we have decided to organize the lecture along the lines of a debate, we might use the introduction to set forth the topic to be debated, explaining why it is an important issue.

In addition to capturing the audience's attention and setting in motion the flow of the lecture, some lecturers try to carry out another task in the introduction: set induction. Set induction is an educational technique in which the lecturer helps the students recall information and ready thinking skills they will need to process any new information in the lecture. It is similar to the command: "Get ready. . . . Get set. . . . Go!"[13] The "get set" alerts the runners to the fact that the race is about to begin. Set induction is a brief review of material covered in past classes or a recalling of information the audience already possesses. It helps students get ready for the rest of the lecture.

Some examples may be helpful: "Last week we covered . . . This morning we are going one step further by . . ." or "Most of you know the story of——in the Bible. Let's see if we can remember it as a class. . . . Over the years, the church's greatest theologians have looked at this story in different ways. Today, we are going to examine some of them." Set induction helps students review ideas previously covered in class or retrieve knowledge they already possess and link it to the new information presented in the lecture. This allows them to build on the foundation they already have, creating a much better chance the lecture material will be stored in long-term memory.

To summarize, many good lecturers try to do two things in their introductions: get their students' attention and set in motion the flow of the lecture based on an organizing principle. In addition, many also use set induction to help students bring to mind the relevant background knowledge they already possess. These goals can be put in the form of several questions: How can I get my class's attention as I begin the lecture? How can I set in motion everything else that follows? What background knowledge should I help them bring to mind as I begin the lecture?

The Body of the Lecture

The body of the presentation outline builds on the introduction and follows the pattern set by the organizing principle. The body should be divided into distinct parts. Let's say we have decided to lecture on questions contemporary Presbyterians raise about the traditional doctrine of predestination, a doctrine in which God is viewed as deciding on the salvation of some and the damnation of others in eternity. In the introduction we present two examples of this doctrine found in the denomination's confessions. The body of the lecture is divided into three questions many modern people have about this doctrine: (1) Does not this doctrine undercut human freedom? (2) Does it not make God an arbitrary despot? (3) Is there clear evidence for it in the Bible? Part one of the body of the lecture deals with question one; part two, with question two; and part three, with question three.

The body of the lecture flows out of the introduction and follows the pattern of the organizing principle. It should be clear by now why our decision about the organizing principle is such an important part of our planning. The same material covered in the lecture just outlined above could be organized in a number of different ways, depending on the organizing principle.

For example, the lecture could easily be organized along the lines of a debate. The introduction might present the doctrine as something that should be debated by contemporary Presbyterians, pointing out the problems many modern people have with this doctrine. The body then might be divided into two basic parts, each presenting a different side of the debate. The points noted above could serve as one side of the debate and the following points might represent the other side: (1) Human beings are bound by life's circumstances far more than they are free to choose how they live; (2) God's ways are not our ways and whether or not the doctrine of predestination offends modern thinking is really not the point; and (3) There is more evidence for this doctrine in scripture than meets the eye, at least the great theologians Augustine, Calvin, and Luther thought so. In contrast to an organizing principle governed by three questions, this lecture's body would have two basic parts structured along the lines of a debate. Each side of the debate would have three subpoints.

The body of the lecture, then, follows an organizing principle. The basic points that were kept in the idea outline are now organized in terms of the pattern followed in the presentation. In moving from the idea outline to the body of the presentation outline, it is often helpful to begin by creating a general skeleton of the presentation outline first, writing down the basic points to be covered. Then subpoints and examples are added. Since examples are so important, we will give them special attention later.

As we create the body of the presentation outline, we need to consider not only the ideas to cover but also how to present them. This means reflecting on the delivery of the lecture. Keep in mind what has already been said about students' attention span. We will have to work hard to keep their attention during the lecture. For this reason, it is crucial to plan for diversity of presentation within the lecture. A good rule of thumb is "Never do any single thing for very long." Think in terms of changing the presentation format about every ten minutes.[14]

This can take place in a variety of ways. One important way is to alter periodically the content of the lecture. If we have been focusing primarily on explaining an idea, then shift to a story or illustration. Another important way of altering the presentation is to ask students a question or pause to allow them to ask questions and make comments. The use of audiovisuals at various points in a lecture also creates variety. Pausing to listen to a brief audio tape or to view a section of video tape can help keep the class's attention.

Physical movement during the lecture also brings variety to the presentation. Writing ideas on a blackboard or newsprint has the effect of drawing attention to the point we are making. Many good lecturers do not present the outline of their lecture to students in advance. They reveal it as they go along by writing each important point on the board as they come to it. Going to the board or newsprint and writing down each point breaks up the monotony that comes from a lecture given by someone standing in the same place for a prolonged period of time. Some lecturers like to move about the room when they field questions, shifting to the front of the lectern or jotting down comments on the board.

It helps to plan for this kind of variation in the presentation outline. Many teachers write themselves instructions about their delivery under the idea that will be covered at that point in the lecture. Some even like to underline or use a different color pen for their "delivery instructions" to make them easier to see during the lecture. If they plan to use a blackboard or newsprint, they attempt to visualize how they want it to look at the end of the session.

Periodic Summaries

The third part of a lecture involves periodic summaries and transitional statements. These elements are key links between each part of a lecture. The summaries review, in capsule form, the material just covered and point to the material that comes next. They are like brief timeouts taken during a basketball game. The players can rest for a minute while the coach reviews what has been going on and explains what the players should do when the game resumes.

Giving students a chance to rest briefly and listen to a summary at different points during a lecture allows them to catch up if their attention has wandered or to correct misunderstandings of the material. It also signals that one part of the lecture is completed and another part will begin.

When offering a summary, we should avoid adding new information. Our goal is to review briefly the material covered already. Sometimes it makes sense simply to review the last point presented. At other times, relating the point just covered to the ideas presented before it is in order. This keeps before students a skeletal outline of the lecture as it unfolds.

We do not always have to offer the summaries ourselves. Sometimes, the students can be asked to summarize the material just covered. This gives teachers some sense of what their students have understood. It also gives the class a chance to hear the material summarized in words other than the lecturer's.

If an outline of the lecture has been placed on the blackboard or newsprint, it is helpful to refer to this while summarizing. Consider moving physically to the board or newsprint to add variety to the presentation. It would then be easy to jot down the next point to be covered.

Many times, transitional statements are part of the periodic summaries. After indicating what the focus has been in the lecture and signaling a shift to a new point, the transitional statement tells something about how the new point is related to the material already covered.

These statements are more important than most people realize, and we should pay special attention to the way they are phrased. Many people find it helpful to write out their transitional statements word for word in their presentation outlines. Consider how important clear directions are when you travel to a place you have never visited before. The wording of transitional statements, likewise, should be clear, allowing students to know where they will be going in the next part of the lecture.

It is also helpful to let students know the relationship between where they have been and where they are going next. For example, if the new point is one of a series of points, we should indicate this fact: "Still another point of importance is . . ." or "This leads us to yet one more area . . ." In contrast, if our next point deals with the consequences of the material just covered, our transitional statement should indicate this: "As a result of . . ." or "We come now to the consequences of what we have just examined."

Different parts of a lecture can be related in many ways. Our job in a transitional statement is to send a clear signal to students about what, in the case of our lecture, this relationship is. Doing this serves as a kind of "sneak preview" that tells our students how to understand the material we are about to present.

The Conclusion

The conclusion of a lecture provides students with the sense that the lecture has reached a destination. This is often hard to achieve in a church school class, as children begin to knock on the door or class members slip out to go to choir. It is easy for a lecture simply to peter out. However, creating a sense of the ending is important. It represents the final impression the class is left with.

Consider how important the ending of a movie is. Sometimes, the good guys win or the mystery is solved. The audience leaves the theater laughing and in good spirits. At other times, the movie ends on a tragic note, and the audience leaves in virtual silence or even in tears. While the conclusion of a lecture is not necessarily this dramatic, it does create a final, and often long-lasting, impression.

Conclusions, like movie endings, can take a variety of different forms. They can provide the class with a clear sense it has reached a destination by offering the culminating insight of the lecture. Or conclusions can provide the class with a final summary of the lecture, reviewing the main points. Or they can leave the class with a sense that the lecture has only scratched the surface of the subject and that much more could be said. Conclusions can serve a variety of purposes, depending on the way the lecture has been organized and the final impression we want to create.

In the church, where attendance of most educational activities is voluntary, it is often important for us to pique our class members' curiosity through conclusions that motivate them to come back. This can be done in a variety of ways. We can leave them with a series of questions the lecture has left unanswered, telling them we will begin the next meeting by asking for their thoughts on these unresolved issues. Or we can invite them to look for one of two ways that the material covered in the lecture relates to their lives during the coming week. Or we can invite them to select a news event during the coming week that they believe is relevant to the topic of the next session. Depending on how well we know our students, we can ask one or two of them to be prepared to share thoughts at the beginning of the next class. In each case, we have concluded the lecture by inviting students to take the material "out of the classroom" and created an expectation for the following meeting.

Steps in Planning a Lecture

It may be helpful to provide a summary of the various steps involved in planning a lecture. Remember, these are only suggestions and must be tailored to each teacher's unique gifts, approach to planning, and style of teaching. These steps represent less a foolproof path to be followed than an account of ideas that others have found helpful.

1. Read background material, marking the reading or taking notes.
2. Write an idea outline.
   —Scan the material that has been read.

—Write down the important ideas.
—Decide which ideas to keep:
  How much time is available?
  Which ideas did the reading material emphasize?
  Which ideas does the class need to encounter?
  Which ideas do you care about deeply?
3. Write a presentation outline.
  —Reflect on the background knowledge of the students:
    What ideas about the topic do they already have?
    What do they know about it in their life experience?
  —Decide on an organizing principle.
  —Outline the body:
    Follow the organizing principle.
    Include delivery instructions to ensure variety.
  —Write out periodic summaries and transitional statements.
  —Outline the conclusion:
    What is the final impression the lecture is to create?
    How can the lecture be taken "out of the classroom"?
    Are there connections with the next session?

Practicing Our Delivery

Once we have created a presentation outline, much of our preparation is done. The only preparation that remains is practicing our delivery. Some persons like to talk through the lecture prior to giving it. If they are lecturing to a large group and are nervous, they find it helpful to practice the lecture so they can feel more confident. One technique often used in practicing a lecture is to deliver it in the face of some background noise (T.V. or radio). This can be very distracting! If a lecture can be delivered under these circumstances, chances are good it can be delivered without a hitch in class.

Most of the time repeated practice is not necessary. In fact, there is much to be said for the spontaneity that comes from delivering a lecture that has not been practiced again and again. It is probably a good idea to talk through the introduction, conclusion, and summary/transitional statements. If we have these clearly in mind, then the rest of the lecture can be delivered spontaneously if we have a good presentation outline.

Some educational theorists have argued that a lecture is similar to a dramatic presentation.[15] Both require theatrical flair and stage presence. If this were the case, most of us would be doomed from the outset. I believe dramatic presentation is much less important than the ability to communicate our knowledge of and conviction about the subject of the lecture. In preparing lectures, it is good to ask again and again why we care about this material. Then, in the delivery of the lecture, we should try to let our interest and conviction show. If we cannot generate any authentic enthusiasm for the subject, then we probably should consider changing topics. It is hard enough to keep students' attention. Unless we can honestly communicate interest in the subject, then it will be very difficult to spark interest in our hearers.

Feedback During the Lecture

As we gain experience lecturing, we learn to pay attention to the feedback students give us during the lecture. Some of the most important feedback is nonverbal. If our students begin to shift in their chairs or repeatedly clear their throats, then it is time to make a shift in our presentation. When they get a glazed look in their eyes, a wake-up call is clearly in order. Consider

stopping and asking a question or shifting to a story or
illustration. We must make a mid-course correction if
we are to recapture our students' attention.

Some lecturers encourage verbal feedback while lecturing by asking questions such as: "Am I going too
fast?" or "Does this make sense?" or "Are you with me
so far?" Others carry on a kind of running joke with the
people on the back row: "Are you folks still awake?" or
"How about it, back row people, has the coffee begun
to wear off?"[16] This sort of banter, of course, works best
if we have good rapport with our students.

Examples

Two general matters will conclude this discussion of
the lecture: the importance of combining the lecture
with other teaching methods and the importance of
using good examples. Let us begin with the second.

Good examples are crucial to good lecturing. We
should probably spend almost as much time thinking of
good examples as thinking about the basic points we will
cover in the presentation outline. Why are examples so
important? They serve as a link between the lecture
material and the life of our students. Examples are
extremely important in helping students grasp new ideas
and relate these ideas to their lives. Story-examples,
moreover, touch the feelings of our students in ways
that pure concepts cannot.

Good examples do not have a "tacked on" feel to
them. They deepen students' understanding of a lecture's basic points. Often, when we are generating the
idea outline, examples will spontaneously occur to us.
Most of the time, however, we will have to work hard to

come up with good ones. Many experienced teachers have found that examples and illustrations tend to come to them in three somewhat different ways.

One way is when they consciously set out to find an example. Usually, I spend some time after I have my presentation outline in place trying to think of appropriate examples. I begin by identifying the key point I am trying to get across and then look for something in the experience of my audience similar to this point. This is a good time to recall the background knowledge of the students. The example should create a bridge between experience or knowledge with which the students are familiar and the new ideas with which they are unfamiliar.

I once heard a lecturer compare political ideologies to after-shave lotion. "If you take a bit out and splash it on, it's bracing," he said. "But swallow the whole thing, and it can kill you." The example is homely, to be sure. But it was effective, taking something from ordinary experience and using it to help the audience better grasp the point: Ideologies are finite tools of understanding which become dangerous when turned into creeds that are followed fanatically.

A second way many teachers come up with examples is to look for them as they read magazines, books, and newspapers or watch television. The best preachers and public speakers always have their antennae out for good examples. If we prepare far enough in advance, we will be amazed at how many examples "find" us.

A third way of finding examples is more indirect. Creativity often is an unconscious process. If we work at creating the presentation outline, leave it alone, and then come back to it after a day or so, frequently examples seem to emerge out of nowhere. Our uncon-

scious mind has mulled over the ideas we are presenting
and has begun to make connections with other ideas and
experiences. These examples are often the richest and
most emotionally powerful.

Combining the Lecture with Other Methods

As has been pointed out repeatedly, lecturing is extremely difficult, especially in an era dominated by
television. Unless we are an exceptional lecturer, sustaining the interest of our class on a steady diet of
lecturing will be difficult. In the church, people can vote
with their feet. If they do not like our teaching, they will
go elsewhere.

It is not a good idea to lecture every week. Not only is
it very hard to do, but other teaching methods are better
at stimulating students toward more active thinking.
Think in terms of combining the lecture with other
teaching approaches. One week lecture; the next lead a
discussion or organize a panel response.

Consider also combining a lecture with other teaching
methods in the same session. Combining lecture and
discussion can be especially fruitful. For example, plan
for a period in the midst of the lecture when the class
deals with a preplanned question. Or spend the first half
of the class lecturing on a topic and the last half discussing it. This is especially useful when students are not
expected to do any reading in preparation for class. The
lecture introduces them to new material, setting the
stage for an informed discussion. Another approach is
to present one side of a highly charged issue in the
lecture and arrange for one or two class members to give
a rebuttal. In each case, the lecture is combined with

another teaching method, ensuring variety and greater student participation.

Perhaps the most important reason to view the lecture as only one method of teaching among many is the central thesis of this book: <u>If we would create a context</u> <u>in which faith can be awakened, supported, and chal-</u><u>lenged, then we must use a variety of teaching methods.</u> The transmission of knowledge, upon which students can build their beliefs, addresses only one side of the faith cube. Focusing exclusively upon the transmission of knowledge diminishes students' chances of growing in other areas. It is to a second dimension of faith, the relational dimension, we now turn.

4

Teaching for Relationship:
Leading a Discussion

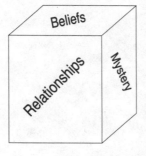

Faith is a relationship of trust in God whose loving-kindness and faithfulness have been shown in Jesus Christ. One of the most important sides of the faith cube is the relationship Christians form with the living God. Faith is not merely holding certain ideas about God. Nor is it merely pursuing certain moral obligations. It is a dynamic, personal relationship with the living God.

In our teaching, we must find ways to help people grow in their relationship with God. The church, of course, does this in a wide variety of ways. Whenever it gathers for worship and the preaching of the Word takes place and the sacraments are administered, grace is communicated to those whose hearts and minds are open. In its informal fellowship—its church dinners, coffee hours, committee work, and acts of mutual care—the church also helps people grow in their relationship with God. The same is true in times of service, when Christians gather to work in soup kitchens or spend time in night shelters.

The teaching ministry is only one of many ways the relational side of the faith cube receives support in the church. We should not underestimate the importance of our teaching, however. There is evidence of a close connection between the quality of a congregation's educational program and the ongoing growth of its members.[1] We must strive to create opportunities in our class for the kind of supportive and challenging sharing that helps people grow in their relationship with God.

Over the past decade, there has been a resurgence of interest in supporting the spirituality of the members of the church. A wide range of teaching approaches have emerged that attempt to help persons grow in their relationship with God. Some of these have focused on developing a regular personal devotional life. Others have focused on small group Bible studies and on covenant discipleship groups. All of these approaches have something to offer us in creating a context in which the relational dimension of faith is addressed.

In this chapter, we will focus on learning how to lead a discussion. While this is only one of many ways the relational dimension of faith can be addressed in our teaching, it is an important one. It is through the give and take of discussion that students move from being relatively passive recipients of knowledge to becoming active contributors in a community of learning. In their conversation with one another, they are given the chance to share their thoughts and feelings and receive those of others. Moments of genuine honesty and self-disclosure can take place that help them grow in their relationship with God. Participation in this kind of community is crucial to a vital faith.

Our task as teachers is to learn how to foster the give and take of genuine conversation in our class. This means that we must acquire understanding and skills in leading discussion. This is one of the more important ways the relational side of the faith cube can receive support in our teaching.

Different Types of Questions

Probably the single most important skill involved in leading a discussion is asking good questions. Questions get a discussion started and keep it going. Different types of questions call for different kinds of thinking. We can improve our ability to lead a discussion by developing a sense of how to form good questions and how to use them in the give and take of a conversation.

Over the years, different ways of classifying questions have been created. I have found the following to be helpful.[2]

Factual Questions

This type of question asks for information. Sometimes this information is stored in students' memories. At other times, we are asking students to look closely at something, such as a Bible passage or a video tape, in order to note certain facts. Some examples of factual questions are

- Who was Jesus' mother?
- Where was Jesus born?
- What does the word *gospel* mean?

- Does Paul ever use the word *gospel* in his letters?
- In Acts 5:4, Peter tells Ananias that he has lied, not just to his fellow Christians, but to whom?

Factual questions are usually the narrowest ones we can ask. They have a single right answer. It is difficult to get a good discussion going on the basis of factual questions alone. Unfortunately, over fifty percent of the questions asked by teachers tend to be of this sort.[3] It is important to learn how to ask for more than the facts.

This does not mean, however, that we should underestimate the importance of helping students retrieve or note information accurately. For example, it often is important to call a Bible study group back to what the text being discussed actually says, especially when an individual has gotten off on some tangent. It is also a good way of getting a discussion started, for sharing facts is usually not as difficult or as threatening as offering opinions or insights about a given topic.

Analytical Questions

This type of question asks students to analyze a certain body of information and draw conclusions about it. We as teachers have in mind the right answer or at least a range of possible right answers. We are asking students to go beyond a simple recall of the facts to an analysis of what these facts mean. We are engaging them in an active process of thinking in which they see relationships the facts alone do not provide. The following are some examples of analytical questions:

- Can you list three characteristics of the kingdom of God found in both Bible passages we studied today?

• In light of what we have seen thus far, what is the role of "the poor" in the Gospel of Luke?

• What are some of the differences between infant baptism and believers' baptism?

• What themes is Paul introducing in the greeting of his letter to the Romans?

• What are some of the differences between catechetical instruction as practiced during the days of Luther and Calvin and confirmation as practiced in many modern churches?

Many times the analytical question builds directly on the information attained through factual questions. Once we have gotten students to note certain facts, we then invite them to draw conclusions on the basis of these facts. Since we are asking them to come up with certain conclusions, it is important for us to think through the answers to these questions in advance.

Analytical questions frequently take more time to answer than factual questions. This is because they demand active thinking. We should be prepared for longer pauses after we ask them. We need to give students enough time to do some thinking and not cut them short.

Productive Questions

Another type of question asks students to come up with their own answers. The productive question is open-ended and does not seek a correct answer. On the basis of students' creativity and imagination, they are to come up with their own unique responses. In short, they are asked to "produce" something that is genuinely new. Some examples of productive questions are

- What are some different ways people come to know Christ? How did you come to know Christ?
- In what ways is the church today like the church Paul was addressing in his letter to the Corinthians?
- Can people who are not Christians go to heaven?
- What role should the church play in American politics today?

There is no single right answer to any of these questions. We are asking students to "produce" answers that are genuinely their own. It is helpful if students can support their answer with facts and analysis, but these in themselves are not enough. Students must make a creative leap to come up with their answers.

Many questions that focus on relating the Bible or theology to our students' lives are productive questions. There are no right answers. They must creatively link knowledge they have gained through study with the particular circumstances of their own lives. When you teach, frame questions that provoke insight and thinking. Communicate that there are no wrong answers to these questions and affirm the answers that are given.

Evaluative Questions

Evaluative questions ask students to make a value judgment about something. There are no right answers here, either. Like productive questions, evaluative questions are fairly broad and open-ended. Students are to use a standard to evaluate something. The following are examples of evaluative questions:

- What are the most important teachings of the Bible?
- What makes a minister a good minister?

- Do you think the American church is doing all that it can to fight world hunger? Explain.
- Is it possible to be a good Christian and an effective politician at the same time? Why or why not?
- Is it good or bad that many African churches have introduced traditional African singing, drumming, and dancing into their worship in recent years?

Obviously, there are no right answers to these questions. We are asking our students to evaluate something. To do so, they must use some sort of standard to judge whether it is good or bad, right or wrong, healthy or unhealthy.

In the first question above, for example, students are asked to decide which teachings of the Bible are the "most important." To answer this, they must do two things. First, they must recall the basic teachings of the Bible. Second, they must decide what "most important" means, forming a standard by which to judge the various teachings of the Bible.

For instance, some people might argue that justification by grace through faith is the core of the Bible and judge all of its teachings with this standard. On this basis, Martin Luther felt that the epistle of James, which stresses good works, was of lesser value than the book of Romans. Others might stress God's liberating work in freeing people from oppression as the most important teaching of the Bible. Those portions which stress the subordination of slaves or women would be seen as reflecting the worldly standards of the day and less important than other portions of the Bible.

Evaluative questions are not easy to answer, and we must give our students time to think. They also can spark interesting discussions in class, sometimes even heated discussions, and can help students reflect on the standard they use to make their judgments. Many times the standard used to evaluate something is held at an unconscious level. One of the most rewarding parts of teaching is helping people become aware of the standards they hold, allowing them to examine these standards critically in a supportive, caring environment.

Leading a Discussion: General Comments

Many people find leading a discussion based on questions far more frightening than standing up in front of a group and delivering a lecture. This is because of the spontaneity and unpredictability involved in leading a discussion. A lecturer has far greater control over the class than a discussion leader. We can prepare for a discussion in advance but enter an exciting, unpredictable world once the discussion actually begins.

Many of us who teach may wonder if we are up to the task. The teacher, however, is only partially responsible for how the discussion goes. Students may refuse to do the assigned reading or be unwilling to offer their opinions. Perhaps they never have been encouraged to share their own thoughts and feelings before. Sometimes even excellent teachers simply cannot get a good discussion going with a particular group.

What follows are suggestions that may be helpful in creating a context in which a good discussion can take place. Once more, we must remember that there is no foolproof approach that will work for all teachers. These ideas must be taken and adapted to each teacher's own gifts and situation.

Planning for Discussion

Much of the planning depends on the type of discussion we decide to lead. Different types of discussion will be examined in depth later. For now, it is enough to point out the importance of keeping in mind the different types of questions. Remember, most teachers ask far more factual questions than they should. We should plan to ask a number of different types of questions in order to engage our students in different types of thinking. We should try to avoid questions that can be answered with a simple "Yes" or "No."

Getting a Discussion Started

In general, it is a good idea to start with questions that are fairly easy and nonthreatening. Factual questions are much easier to answer than evaluative questions, for example. No one likes to come into a class and suddenly be asked a question that invites them to share something personal or that takes a great deal of thought. Most of the time, it is good to ease our students into the discussion.

I had a professor of preaching who once described the rhythms of a sermon in a way that is also applicable to the flow of a discussion: Start slow, go low, strike fire, retire. Ideally, we should ease our students into a discussion, invite them to do some solid thinking and sharing, build toward culminating insights, and quickly tie things together with a conclusion. Unfortunately, the flow of a discussion cannot be controlled as easily as that of a sermon.

Moreover, there are exceptions to every rule. Sometimes, beginning with a dramatic, controversial question that stirs the class up can be quite effective. Bang! We jump right into the discussion. Questions like these might get the attention of a class:

- Some people argue that we are far more likely to confess our racism than our sexism. Do you agree with this line of thought? If so, why? If not, why not?
- Most people in the church want to avoid conflict at all costs. Do you think this is a true statement? If so, why do we avoid conflict in the church?
- "It is easier for a camel to go through the eye of a needle than for someone who is rich to enter the kingdom of God" (Luke 18:25). Why is this Bible verse of special relevance to Americans today?

Starting off with such intensity is risky. Students may not be ready to jump right in. We might be left with a long, uneasy silence or a few superficial remarks. Even if we are successful in getting a good discussion going, it may be difficult to build on it over a period of time. When we start with a bang, there is a tendency for the discussion to peter out. In general, it is a good rule to "start slow and go low." There are exceptions to every rule, however, and one of the keys to leading a good discussion is our willingness to take risks.

Using Silence

Many teachers are afraid of silence in the classroom. There is nothing more threatening than asking a question and having no one respond. This can produce a knot in the stomach pretty quickly. Many times, how-

ever, the silence is much shorter than we think. Some
research indicates that teachers wait an average of only
one second for students to answer their questions.[4] This
research also indicates that when teachers wait from
three to five seconds, more answers of better quality are
given. We should try to become aware of how long we
tend to wait after asking a question. Remember, we
have just asked our students to think. We need to give
them a chance to do so.

One technique is to count slowly to ten after asking a
question.[5] If no answer is forthcoming, then we might
rephrase the question in a simpler form. We should try
to pay attention to the nonverbal signals we are sending
our class. If we are standing up, we might go to a solid
object, like a wall or podium and lean against it. This
tells the class we are comfortable and can wait indefi-
nitely. We might try making eye contact with different
people around the room and offer facial gestures
or body motions that say to the class, "Can anyone
respond?"

If we still get no response, we might say something
like: "I'm not sure what this silence means. Have I
asked a question that doesn't make sense to you or are
you still thinking?" Then wait again. Or we might say,
"Could one of you share with the class what you hear me
asking? Apparently, my question is unclear." Another
approach is to invite the students to turn to their neighbor and respond to the question. Then, in an open-
ended way, ask if anyone is willing to share his or her
insights with the entire class.

It is tempting to do one of two things when we are
confronted with silence after asking a question: answer
the question for the class or ask two or three new

questions. Neither is a helpful way of dealing with silence.

The important point to remember is that silence is our friend in the classroom. It is an open space for thinking and recollection. We need to learn to master our anxiety over silence and use it to our advantage in our teaching. Few things communicate greater confidence in a class than a teacher's willingness to give it time to mull over a question that cannot be responded to immediately.

Keeping a Discussion Going

A number of techniques can be used to keep a discussion going once we have gotten it started. Here are some of the more important ones.

Affirm student responses. Few things are more important to keeping a discussion going than showing our students we have listened to and valued their responses. Most of the time, even wrong answers should receive some sort of praise, for the student risked sharing his or her opinion. This is especially important during the initial part of a discussion. If we summarize and affirm the answers given in the first part of the discussion, students learn they can share their responses safely. An atmosphere is created in which discussion can flourish.

Avoid the mini-lecture. Nothing can kill a discussion quicker than a teacher who interjects a mini-lecture in response to a student's answer. It is especially important to avoid this when we are trying to get the discussion going. It is more important to promote involvement than to use students' answers as an opportunity to give our own lengthy response. There are exceptions to this rule, of course. Sometimes our preparation for class has given us access to information that others may not have. Sharing this can help the discussion reach a deeper level. We must remember, however, that even at these points we are a resource for the class, not the ultimate authority who knows all the right answers. Our job is to facilitate discussion, not to provide the key insights.

Ask prompting questions. Prompting questions are asked when the class or a particular student is unable to come up with an answer. They are questions that provide clues or hints that help the student out. Generally, they are a more focused version of the question that has just been asked. Suppose we have asked: "Can you list three characteristics of the kingdom of God found in both Bible passages studied today?" and no one responds. A prompting question might be: "Look at verse seven in the Matthew passage and verse twelve in the Luke passage. What do they have in common?" Prompting questions "prime the pump" and help students begin to formulate an answer themselves.

Ask probing questions. Probing questions invite the student to go deeper than his or her initial response. Sometimes this involves shifting from one type of question to another. In a Bible study focusing on Matthew, we might ask a factual question like: "Where was Jesus born?" and then shift in our probing question to an analytical question like, "Why is it important that the author quotes the Old Testament to show that the Messiah would come out of Bethlehem?" The shift from a factual to an analytical question is used to introduce the theme of promise and fulfillment that is so central to Matthew. Sometimes probing questions simply build on the answer that has been given and invite the student to think about why he or she gave this answer. An evaluative question like "What makes a minister a good minister?" might be probed with questions that invite respondents to identify the origin of their images of a good minister. Asking good probing questions is an important skill to learn.

Redirect the discussion for greater participation. This technique involves shifting the discussion away from the answer given by one student and inviting others to respond. We might simply ask general questions of the class like "What do the rest of you think of Jane's response?" or "What are some other ways of thinking about this?" Sometimes we redirect the discussion to specific students by calling on them directly: "Tom, what do you think of this issue?" We must know our students well to be able to do this, however. Some students feel threatened by being called on and might stop coming to class if this is done on a regular basis.

Give qualifying instructions as the flow of the discussion is redirected. We greatly influence what goes on in a discussion through the qualifying instructions we give as we redirect the flow of the conversation from one person to another. We influence the kind of responses we are likely to get and the general tone of the discussion. If we are trying to provoke debate, for example, our qualifying instructions can make this clear, asking for the other side of an issue: "Who disagrees with Jane's response?" or "Paul, you seemed to be moving in a different direction earlier today. Do you agree with Jane?" Sometimes, we can redirect the discussion in a way that asks for synthesis: "We have looked at different sides of this issue. What are some common themes?" or "We emphasized the differences, who sees similarities?"

Use qualifying instructions for other purposes. We can influence the flow of the discussion in other ways through the qualifying instructions we give in our questions. We can influence the pace of the discussion, speeding it up or slowing it down. We can pick up the pace by asking: "Quickly, as many of you as possible, what is your impression of this passage?" or "In a few short words, what do you remember from last week?" We can slow it down by including instructions like the following: "Let's ponder this for a moment and ask what it really means to us today" or "Take your time and think before answering. . . ." We also can influence how concrete or abstract the discussion is: "Give specific examples of this in the church today" or "If you were to generalize about what we've been discussing, what would you say?"

Bringing a Discussion to a Close

It is not always easy to bring a discussion to a nice, neat resolution. That is not necessarily our goal. Sometimes the different ideas and feelings that have been shared stand as a reminder that the church is not made up of people who are just alike. Everyone does not come to the end of the discussion with the same conclusion. The issue is not completely resolved!

While resolving the discussion is not always important, it is important to create a sense of closure. Not everyone in the church values the exchange of ideas and feelings that lies at the heart of discussion. Sometimes they view it as little more than "sharing ignorance." Bringing closure to the discussion can help create a sense that the conversation has arrived somewhere. It also can remind the participants of the ground they have covered.

There are a variety of ways to bring closure to a discussion. Many teachers like to warn their students about ten minutes before the class is to end. This encourages people who have something pressing to share to jump in. It also signals that the discussion is about to wind down. Another way of providing closure is to offer a summary. This can be given by the teacher or one of the members of the class. If an outline or key ideas have been written on the board or newsprint, the summary can refer to these. Another way of providing closure is to ask class members to select one thing they have learned from the discussion and to let as many people as possible share their insights briefly. A similar technique is to ask the class to share unresolved issues or questions. These might even point toward issues to be dealt with in the next class.

A sense of closure is important. There is nothing worse than having a discussion end abruptly as the bell rings or when children knock on the door. People begin to leave while the teacher or a class member is in mid-sentence. We need to be sure to leave enough time at the end of class to draw the discussion to a close. Five to seven minutes is a good rule of thumb. Even longer might be needed if we are asking the members of the entire class to share their insights.

Different Types of Discussion

One of the more important decisions we make when
planning for a discussion is the type of discussion we
want to lead. It is helpful to think of the types as being
on a continuum. A continuum arranges similar items in
an orderly sequence. Imagine the color white, for example, at one end of a line and the color black at the other
end. In between are various shades of white, gray, and
black, gradually moving from the lighter colors near the
white end to darker colors as the black end is approached. The continuum contains a wide range of
shades between the two endpoints.

Different types of discussion can be pictured in the
same way. At one end of the continuum is *focused
discussion*. In this type, the teacher has a clear idea of
where he or she would like the discussion to go and
attempts to move it in that direction. The goal is to
cover a certain amount of material and help students
assimilate it. At the other end is *open-ended discussion*.
In this type, the flow of the discussion emerges out of
the sharing of the class, not the plan of the teacher. The
teacher is primarily responsible for planning thought-
provoking questions and helping move the conversation
along. He or she does not attempt to guide it toward
predefined goals.

Many of our discussion classes in the church fall somewhere between these two ends of the continuum. They
can be referred to as *mixed discussions*. Sometimes, the
teacher has a clear plan in mind but is ready to deviate
from that plan if meaningful conversation begins to go in
an unanticipated direction. This remains closer to the
focused discussion end of the continuum. At other times,

the teacher offers a mini-lecture and then moves into an open-ended discussion. Obviously, this is closer to the other end of the continuum. A mixture of planning, guidance, and spontaneity places the discussion somewhere near the middle of the continuum.

Each of these different types of discussion calls for somewhat different forms of planning. They also take somewhat different skills. Leading an open-ended discussion involves the ability to think on our feet as the discussion unfolds. We must intuitively sense if a line of thought is going somewhere that is fruitful or merely following the interests of one student. We also must be able to relate the discussion spontaneously back to the topic being studied. A focused discussion involves the ability to plan ahead. We must write good questions in advance and anticipate the class's responses in order to project possible follow-up questions. Much less spontaneity is required. Planning for each type of discussion follows somewhat different lines.

Planning for a Focused Discussion

This type of discussion is only one step away from a lecture, and planning for it is almost identical to the steps outlined in the previous chapter.[6] We begin by reading the material we are going to discuss, and then go back over it to select the central points that make up our idea outline. We then form the general skeleton of a presentation outline by ordering these ideas in terms of an organizing principle.

It is at this point that our planning begins to deviate from that used in preparing for a lecture. Our next step is to turn the presentation outline into a discussion outline. This consists of questions that correspond to each of the points covered in the outline. Instead of presenting these points as we would in a lecture, we turn them into questions that guide the flow of the discussion. Our goal is to form a discussion outline with major questions and subquestions that are as detailed as a lecture. It is this outline that we will follow in leading the discussion.

Suppose we are teaching a class in a white, middle-class church. The class is studying a book on world hunger and the church's response. Everyone is to have read the first three chapters before class. The basic flow of the discussion might be as follows:

I.   Introduction to World Hunger: The Hidden Reality
II.   The Facts About World Hunger
III.   The Biblical Mandate: Serve Those in Need
IV.   Conclusion: Sharing of Thoughts and Feelings About This Material

The task in forming a discussion outline is to translate each of these major points into questions. We then must fill out each major question with subquestions, just as we would create subpoints in a detailed outline for a lecture. The major ideas might translate into questions like the following:

I.   Why do we know so few people who are hungry?
II.   What are the hard, cold facts about the reality of worldwide hunger as presented in our reading?
III.   What does the Bible say about how we should respond? Can we point to specific passages that deal with this topic?
IV.   What are some of the thoughts and feelings that have been stirred up by the reading and discussion? Share them in a few sentences.

Each of these major questions would be followed by additional questions. 'We need to be sure to include different types of questions in the outline. When we have finished creating our outline, it is a good idea to check it over to make sure this is the case. Different types of questions might be used at different points in the discussion.

In the outline given immediately above, for example, we might focus on productive and evaluative questions in the introduction, helping our students reflect on why the reality of world hunger is so far removed from their day-to-day lives. We also might help them recognize the unconscious standards they use to judge street people when they encounter them on their shopping trips in the heart of the city. The second point might shift to factual questions, helping the class recall what the book said about the reality of world hunger. The third point might move from factual questions about Bible passages to analytical questions that lead to generalizations about biblical themes. These might be followed by productive questions that relate these themes to the church today. The final part of the discussion might use an evaluative question, asking the class to reflect on their reactions to the material, noting especially their personal responses to it.

In a focused discussion, we try to anticipate the possible responses of the group and write follow-up questions in the outline. We might even decide whom we are going to call on to answer a particular question. If we know the group well, we will know which person can best handle which type of question and who is willing to jump right in and get the discussion started.

If we choose this type of discussion for the class, then

our basic goal is to get through the plan we have set up. This means we must be quite direct in our guidance of the class. If the discussion gets off track, it is our job to pull it back on course. This does not mean we must thwart all spontaneity. A skillful leader of this type of discussion can make it seem as if the group itself is determining the flow of the discussion. These teachers are able to ask their preplanned questions in a way that builds on student responses. They also can redirect the discussion to get more and more people involved. All the while, they are steadily moving the discussion forward, following their outline. Some teachers even write their outline on the board prior to the discussion or as it unfolds.

The focused discussion is especially good for teachers who find the unpredictability of a discussion frightening. It allows us to have a plan before us. We know what questions to ask and where we would like to end up. This type of discussion is a good place to start if we have no experience leading a discussion.

We should try, however, to move beyond this type of discussion at some point in our teaching. Even if we never feel confident enough to try an open-ended discussion, we still might try leading discussions that are open to greater spontaneity and group direction than a focused discussion. This grants greater power to the class members and allows them to determine the direction that the discussion takes.

A summary of the planning for a focused discussion is as follows:

1. Read the material, marking it or taking notes.
2. Write an idea outline.
3. Write the general points of a presentation outline.

4. Turn the presentation outline into a discussion outline.
—Write out major questions.
—Fill in follow-up questions based on anticipated student responses.
—Consider who to call on to answer questions.
—Decide what points to put on the board.

Planning for an Open-ended Discussion

At first glance, it might seem that less planning is involved in preparing for an open-ended discussion. This is not the case. If anything, we must know our material even better, because we are not certain what direction the discussion is going to move in. We must be ready to go in many different directions!

In an open-ended discussion, we do not attempt to control the flow of the discussion. Our tasks are to get the discussion going, to deepen the insights that emerge as the discussion unfolds, and to include as many members of the class as possible. Perhaps the best way of thinking about this type of discussion is along the lines of a Socratic dialogue.

In ancient Greece, the philosopher Socrates helped his students discover the truth by engaging them in dialogue. Instead of attempting to teach the great truths of life directly, he would pose an issue or let his students pose one and then press them to deeper and deeper understanding through a series of questions. His role as teacher was that of a midwife. He helped deliver the baby, but it was not his own. The truth emerged out of the dialogue.

The same is true in an open-ended discussion. We as teachers are not attempting to communicate certain ideas we have formed in advance. Rather, we are helping our students arrive at the truth themselves. We are midwives, assisting in the process of delivering another's insights. The key to leading this type of discussion is asking probing questions that take the conversation to deeper and deeper levels of understanding.

How can we prepare for this type of discussion? Our initial preparation is very similar to that involved in preparing for a lecture or a focused discussion. We read the material carefully, marking it or taking notes and identifying the important ideas. Our next step, however, is not to turn this into a discussion outline. Rather, it is to engage in a personal, creative mulling over of these ideas in terms of our own life situation. Which idea seems to grab us the most? Why? How does it speak to us? Does it challenge us? Comfort us? It might be helpful to jot down the different thoughts that come to mind as we reflect. We do not need to force these thoughts into a rational pattern. We simply let them percolate up. This is the way creativity often works.

It might be helpful to go through a similar process in relation to several of our students. We might pick two or three people who are very different and visualize them one at a time in our mind. Which ideas are likely to strike them as important? Which ideas do we think are important for them, even if they might not think so? Again, it is often helpful to jot down random thoughts that come to us.

In many ways, this time of reflection is our most important preparation. We are beginning to anticipate how students will respond to certain issues, if they come up in class. It is out of this sort of thinking before class that we will have the ability to respond spontaneously to students' insights.

While we do not attempt to focus an open-ended discussion, it often is helpful to have before us a list of the important ideas that our reflections have suggested to us. Sometimes our students will generate many ideas themselves, and we can simply follow their lead. Sometimes we will have to play a more active role in raising issues. In either case, it is a good idea to have the more important ideas and issues right in front of us. It is often difficult to remember even good ideas once the conversation gets started. We should not feel compelled to cover these ideas, but they are ready at hand if our class has difficulty getting started.

The next step is to decide how to begin the discussion. We can either start the discussion or devise a way of getting the class to take responsibility for the discussion from the beginning. If we choose to start the discussion ourselves, we might use one of the following techniques:

Begin with personal sharing and then invite others to share along the same lines. For example, an open-ended discussion of the hunger book mentioned above might begin with our sharing a personal incident in which we encountered the devastation of hunger firsthand. We might then ask if anyone else has had similar experiences. A natural transition would be to ask why it is so hard to move from these firsthand experiences to the systemic causes of hunger.

Offer two or three issues we think the reading material raises and ask class members to decide which seems the most important to them today. Follow up their responses by asking them why the issues mentioned seem so important.

Ask a broad, evaluative question about the material. Do you think our church does enough to respond to the issue of world hunger? Why or why not?

Alternatively, this type of discussion can be started in a manner that places more of the burden on our students. This is easier to do if they have done some reading in advance. Even if they have not, however, we can draw on their life experience to get them into the topic. The following are some possibilities:

Ask them to share feelings that were stirred by the reading. "What made you the maddest about this book on hunger? Who was your anger directed toward: yourself, the author, the church, our country? Why?"

Invite them to remember and then share a situation that is connected in some way to the topic to be discussed. "Have you ever lost someone that you were very close to? What sort of feelings did you experience?" After a time of sharing, we might introduce the topic: "Today we are going to discuss how we can minister to people who are grieving. What were some of the things people said or did that were most helpful when you lost someone?"

Have students brainstorm about the important ideas that emerged out of their reading. "In a few words, share one or two of the most important ideas our reading covered." List these on the board or newsprint. Then ask, "Which of these ideas strike you as a good place to begin? Why?"

These are only a few ways we can get a discussion started. When things go well, the discussion will continue on its own. A good beginning makes our job much easier in an open-ended discussion. It is worth spending some quality time planning how to engage our class right from the start.

A summary of the planning involved in an open-ended discussion is as follows:

1. Read the material, marking it or taking notes.
2. Reflect on the material in relation to your life.
   —Jot down thoughts and feelings.
3. Visualize several students.
   —Reflect on how this material is relevant to them.
   —Jot down thoughts and feelings.
4. Create an idea sheet by listing important ideas and issues that occur during your reflection.
5. Write out how you will start the discussion.
   —Write out initial instructions and/or questions.

Planning for Mixed Discussions

By "mixed discussions" I mean those falling somewhere on the continuum between focused and open-ended discussions. Most discussions we lead in the church will be of this sort. It is helpful to decide which end of the continuum we would like the discussion to approach. Are we primarily planning a focused discussion which is open to following quality insights wherever they might lead? Or are we primarily planning an open-ended discussion in which we periodically offer insights from our reading that are relevant to the discussion as it unfolds? Our choice makes a difference in planning and in our leadership of the class.

If the mixed discussion we are planning is closer to the focused end of the continuum, we would do well to compose a question outline in the manner already described. Our actual guidance of the class, however, should be much less direct in a mixed discussion. We should be willing to suspend the outline, if quality conversation begins to emerge around some issue. We should not work as hard at pulling the class back on track to cover everything we have planned. We might even place in our outline productive or evaluative questions that are open-ended enough to go in many different directions. If the discussion takes off at these points, we should let it go. Our goal is quality learning and insight, not getting through the material.

A mixed discussion that tends toward the open-ended variety should be planned along the lines of an open-ended discussion. Often it is different from a purely open-ended discussion because we offer the class input that allows it to carry on the discussion at a deeper level, especially when the class has not done any reading in advance. We might begin by sharing a brief summary of the reading or interject comments about it as the discussion moves along. In this sort of discussion, we should see ourselves as a resource of knowledge as well as a midwife. It is not easy to balance these two roles. We should try not to place ourselves in the position of expert to whom the class looks for the correct answer. Rather, we are offering information that can help them come up with their own insights.

Levels of Sharing in Discussion

People usually grow in their relationship with God only if they are supported and challenged in their relationships with other Christians. For this reason teaching in the church must include discussion. The give and take of discussion can encourage us to develop a richer and more authentic spirituality.

Admittedly, this is not always the case. Much discussion in the church does not reach the level of honesty and self-disclosure that spurs us to grow in our relationship with God. But what is the alternative? By ourselves, we are apt to get caught in a web of self-deception and self-satisfaction. We need others in the church to support us and challenge us on the slow and often painful road toward Christian maturity. Our task as teachers is to make it possible for rich and authentic conversation to take place.

The link between discussion and personal spirituality is perhaps most apparent when we reflect on the different levels of sharing that can take place in a discussion.[7] Four different levels can be identified:

1. Informal chit-chat
2. Sharing of information and ideas
3. Sharing of personal insights and feelings
4. Self-disclosure that makes a person vulnerable

All four levels of sharing have a legitimate place in discussion. It is neither possible nor desirable to move toward personal self-disclosure in every class. Chit-chat is perfectly legitimate in classes where people do not know each other very well or are just beginning to build relationships.

A Matter of Boundaries

Most of the time, the level of sharing that takes place in a discussion is related to the boundaries of the group.

Every time our class gathers, a boundary is formed, separating those who are members of the group from those who are not. In *loosely bounded groups*, the membership is open. Some people come one week; others come the next. People may wander in and out as the class takes place. In *tightly bounded groups*, the membership is closed. It is clear who is a member of the group and who is not. The membership does not shift from meeting to meeting.

Many of our church school classes are loosely bounded. They stay on the first two levels of sharing most of the time and, less frequently, move to the third level. Only rarely do moments of self-disclosure take place. The group boundaries simply are not tight enough to make deep sharing possible.

We need to be sensitive to the level of sharing we realistically can expect from our class. We should not try to force people to share when the setting is not appropriate for it. We should encourage our church to offer alternative classes designed for a deeper level of sharing and growth, if it does not already offer them.

Tightly bounded groups afford this possibility, although they do not guarantee it. Other factors like class size and diversity also enter in. In this type of group, the boundary separating members from nonmembers is clearly defined. There is rarely a change in who takes part in the class and who does not. Such groups develop clear expectations about what the class is gathered to do and how it is going to do it. For example, class attendance, assigned reading, and daily prayer might be required of all participants in a small group Bible study. Honest sharing, moreover, might also be encouraged. Sometimes these expectations are clearly articulated;

sometimes, they simply are understood. In either case, members know when the rules have been violated. If a person does not show up in a tightly bounded group, he or she is missed.

Stages of Group Life in Tightly Bounded Groups

In general, the tighter the boundaries of a group, the more likely that deeper levels of communication will be reached. The reason is obvious. Trust can be built over time, allowing group members to risk sharing more of themselves and their relationship with God. Before we are willing to share much personal information, most of us need to know that we can trust those who receive this information. We need to trust that they will keep it in confidence and that they will provide a helpful response. Tight boundaries create a climate of trust and intimacy in which the deepest levels of communication can be reached.

Admittedly, this is not always the case. Some church school classes are tightly bounded but never get beyond the first two levels of communication. The same people attend year in and year out; newcomers are not really welcome. There is little encouragement for individuals to grow in their relationship with God. In this sort of group, tight boundaries are an obstacle to growth, not a support.

Why is it that some tightly bounded groups achieve a deeper level of sharing than others? One important reason is that groups pass through various stages on the way to deep communication. Some groups pass through all of the stages; others seem to get stuck in a stage. Deep sharing takes place only if the group itself has been willing to grow. These stages have been summarized in a manner that is easy to remember: forming, storming, norming, and performing.[8] I will add a fifth stage: reforming.

During the *forming* stage, group members are getting to know each other. The basic issue dealt with is "in or out." People are sizing each other up and deciding whether or not they want to be part of the group. Many times people feel ambivalent during this stage. They want to be accepted by the group and feel close to others, but they are not sure they can trust the group or want to invest themselves in it.

During this stage members of the group are likely to be most dependent on the leader. They look to the leader to give them guidance and to set the emotional climate of the group. By the end of this stage, the boundaries have tightened. People have committed to the group or they have dropped out. The group has agreed on its purpose and formed the rules by which it will carry out its work.

Calling the second stage a time of *storming* can be misleading. All groups do not pass through a period in which the members openly fight with one another. The basic issue dealt with during this stage, however, is universal to group life. It is the struggle to establish leadership and power in the group. The conflict that is part of this stage can be seen along two lines: conflict between the group and the leader and conflict group members have among themselves.

Conflict with the leader takes place for several reasons. Some of these are healthy and promote the group's growth. Others are not positive. Conflict with the leader can be a welcome step after the dependency of the first stage. Group members are beginning to express their own competence. They too have good ideas and abilities that can help the group. The wise leader is not afraid of this sort of challenge to his or her authority. In fact, he or she encourages a sharing of leadership.

The storming stage, however, is not always positive. Sometimes conflict has to do with an unwillingness to give up unrealistic expectations about the group. Some people may come believing that in this small group Bible study they finally will have all their questions answered. Or they come hoping that this sharing group will, at last, allow them to feel close to other church members. Many times, the leader is the symbol of these expectations. As the group develops and these fantasies are not fulfilled, the group members begin to express their dissatisfaction toward the leader or other group members. If these members can move beyond these fantasies, then this represents a positive step in the group's life. If not, it can keep the group from becoming close.

It is important to be aware of what is going on in a group during the storming stage. Unless a group passes through a period in which leadership is shared among group members and people begin to give up their unrealistic expectations about the group, it will be difficult to achieve honest sharing. An undercurrent of conflict and dissatisfaction will prevent the group from establishing bonds of trust that are the basis of self-disclosure.

The *norming* stage has to do with the development of patterns that characterize the group's life. These are predictable patterns in the way that the group members relate to one another. Some groups, for example, jump right into sharing. Others move toward it gradually. Some groups are quite comfortable with unanswered questions; others have a need for closure at the end of every meeting. During this period, moreover, the group members take on certain roles in the group's life. One person is the talker; another the clockwatcher; still another the joke teller.

It is helpful to view the norming stage as something that begins very early in the group's life and passes through several substages. In a sense, this stage overlaps those described already. Every group must establish fairly quickly certain norms which guide its life together. During the initial, forming stage, the group looks to the leader to help set these norms. A good leader finds a way of balancing the group's need for structure and guidance and its need to influence the patterns that are set up, creating a sense of ownership. During the storming stage, the norms set up initially can be altered radically by the emerging leadership in the group. By then, one hopes, people can be more honest about what they really want from the group.

During the third stage, the norming stage proper, the patterns of group life become more fixed. People are used to playing certain roles in the group. They are comfortable following an established framework. While some variation is allowed in the group, it takes place within the established norms. A feeling of "we-ness" develops. New members have to fit in to the established patterns.

Through each of these substages, the group is deciding the level of sharing that will be appropriate. In a sense, we might say that the focal issue is "near or far" in groups that are designed for sharing. How "near" or close do I want to get to the members of the group? By the time the norming stage is completed, it is difficult to achieve deeper levels of sharing in the group than those that are a part of the group's life already.

The fourth stage is the *performing* stage. Once group norms have been established, the group can focus on the task at hand. It can take for granted the structure and roles that have been set up to carry out its work. If the group is to study the Bible, then it has established a certain way of approaching the Bible and applying it to members' lives. If it is a church committee, then the members know each other and how to work together.

I think it is important to add to these four stages a fifth stage called *reforming*. Typically, this stage is seen as part of the performing stage, but it is important enough to give it special emphasis. The reforming stage is a period of ending or recommitment to the group. Periodically, every group must decide whether it should continue or end. Setting a definite time to make this decision allows group members to keep up a high level of commitment to the group for the designated period and then gracefully leave it, if that is their choice.

If the group decides to end or some of its members decide to drop out, special attention should be paid to the mixed feelings likely to emerge. This is especially important if the group has been close. In a sense, the group should be given a decent burial. There is a season for all things, and people should not feel bad about deciding it is time for the group to end or for them to leave it. It is important to acknowledge this ending by allowing people to share their thoughts and feelings about what the group has meant to them.

If the group decides to continue, this is a time for it to

reform its life. It should consider the following issues: Should new members be added? Should the format shift? Should the leadership be changed in some way? Should people alter the roles they have played in the group? This kind of reform should be scheduled into the life of groups that meet on an ongoing basis. It should be done at least every six months, if not more often. Otherwise, the group is likely to grow stale and die a slow, lingering death.

Personal Sharing in Loosely Bounded Groups

While it is harder, it is not impossible to reach deep levels of sharing in loosely bounded groups. Since many of our church school classes are of this sort, a few words are in order about how this might take place. One important consideration is the size of the group. If the group is large (over twenty members), then the intimacy of small group sharing cannot be achieved in the group as a whole. One way to allow people to share at a deep level is to break them into pairs or small groups.

Often it is best to let members form these groups or pairings themselves. This gives people the chance to get together with whomever they feel comfortable. We might say something like: "Find another person with whom you would feel comfortable sharing something about yourself" or "Form groups of three or four in order to discuss this topic." Once people are in groups or pairs, move gradually from one level of sharing to another. It is much less threatening to share factual information than personal thoughts and feelings. Start with levels of sharing that ask for less and move slowly to levels that invite more.

In large classes, it is often helpful to bring the small groups or pairs back together and give them a chance to share in the total group setting. We should not expect the same level of sharing to be achieved at this point as in a more intimate setting. We might phrase our questions in a way that provides leeway in this regard: "Of the various questions discussed, share one or two insights that occurred to you" or "What was the most important insight that occurred to you?" We are asking for a deeper level of sharing in questions like the following: "Share the most painful memory that came to you during your small group discussion" or "What is the one thing you need to work on most right now in your life?" Even in a large group, meaningful sharing can take place, but student responses to these kinds of questions should be completely voluntary.

If a class is small but the membership shifts from week to week, a modified form of the approach just described might be used. We might begin by dividing the class into pairs or small groups and later invite them back together. Our initial questions when the class regathers might focus directly on sharing what they have just discussed. Suppose the small groups have been discussing patterns of parent-child communication in each person's family. When the total group regathers, we might ask each group to share common themes and/or differences in their families' communication patterns. We might ask what problem areas seemed to emerge.

Our next task is to ask a series of questions dealing with a new but related topic, giving the class a chance to continue sharing on the same level. In other words, we are inviting them to share in the total group on the same level as in their smaller group, but now discussing a new topic. In terms of the example above, we might ask them to identify one or two ways they would like to change their communication with their children. The group might offer different insights about how this might take place after each person shares.

Again, we should not force people to share. Little trust has been built up in loosely bounded groups. Participants should go at their own pace. Even in these groups, however, deep sharing can take place, enriching the quality of learning.

Limits on Leading Discussion

As teachers we have limits. We cannot force a good discussion to take place. Nor can we make our class reach a level of sharing that includes a large amount of self-disclosure. It is like playing a board game. We can set up the board and put all the pieces in their proper places, but ultimately, others have to be willing to play.

Clearly, we as teachers can do much to enhance the possibilities that good discussion will take place. We can learn how to ask good questions and follow them up. We can work hard before class to create a good plan. But ultimately, we must accept the limits on what we can do. There is an element of mystery in all this. We can accept neither all the credit nor all the blame for how things go in a discussion.

In the final analysis, community in the church is a creation of the Holy Spirit. A mysterious mixture of human freedom and divine action determines whether a group of individuals can come together in a way that allows them to become a supportive, challenging community in Christ. Our task as teachers is to serve as a vehicle of the Spirit, knowing full well that we cannot control its work. God acts when and where God will to create Christian community. Our task is to serve, as best we can within our human limitations, as a means by which this community is created. This is the joy and the burden of teaching for relationship.

5

Teaching for Commitment: Reinterpreting Life Stories

In this chapter, we turn to the commitment side of the faith cube. Commitment in faith points to the quality of dedication and devotion a person has in his or her relationship with God. Chances are good that teaching in this area may seem like a greater challenge than teaching for belief or relationship. Lecture and discussion are teaching methods with which most of us are familiar.

The Challenge of Teaching for Commitment

Teaching that invites people to deepen their commitment to God may seem like an area we would just as soon leave to someone else. Is this not the minister's responsibility? Is it not best done in worship or on a retreat? Who am I to invite people to deepen their devotion to God? I am not sure how committed I am myself! I do not feel qualified enough as a teacher to start intruding into my students' lives.

These are legitimate questions and concerns. It would be a shame, however, if they prevented us from seriously considering how we can address the commitment side of the faith cube in our teaching. No persons—be they ministers or Christian educators—feel competent to invite people to a deeper level of commitment. At some point, all of them have come to realize that the processes of growth and change in the Christian life are ultimately in God's hands. What they can do and what we can do is try to place ourselves at God's disposal and create a context in which deeper commitment can take place.

Consider what would be missing from the church if it never gave people a chance to explore the quality of their commitment to God. Would it really matter how much information about the Bible they learned or how close they felt to other people in the church? Without commitment, faith becomes shallow. The church cannot afford to ignore this important side of the faith cube in its teaching, and chances are, we as teachers can make an important contribution in this area.

Teaching for Commitment: A First Look

What does teaching commitment look like? How does it differ from the kind of teaching we have examined already? Perhaps the best way to answer these questions is with a brief story. It focuses on an incident that took place in the third session of a five-week series on Christian parenting my wife and I were leading in our church. For the sake of confidentiality, the details have been altered.

During the first two sessions, we had examined theological understandings of parenting and recent research on child development. In the third session, we were giving people the chance to examine their own parenting styles. The class was divided into small groups that had been working together during each of the previous two weeks. Spouses were separated into different groups. Group members were asked to share one aspect of their parenting style that they would like to change to make it more consistent with their understanding of Christian parenting.

After several people had shared in his group, Paul Johnson told the others how hard it was for him to control his temper while parenting. He had recently married for the second time, and his new family had two teenagers. Paul and the stepchildren seemed to clash from day one. Paul shared how he had been brought up in a family in which the father's word was law. "It was a matter of respect," he said. "My stepchildren don't seem to have any idea of what respect is all about." He went on to say, however, that he really did not believe that the old, authoritarian style was consistent with Christian parenting, especially in the situation he was facing. What he wanted was better understanding and communication. "Maybe a little mutual respect would help," he added. These were themes that had been explored in previous sessions.

This marked a turning point for Paul. He realized that if anything different was going to happen in his new family, he was going to have to change. He spoke with his wife about getting the whole family into counseling, which they did. Things were never perfect in his relationship with his stepchildren, but they did get somewhat better. Paul began to think about his Christian responsibilities as a parent in a new way. He abandoned the authoritarian, heavy-handed model he had inherited from his father and began to view the struggle to forge good communication based on mutual respect as a style of parenting consistent with his faith.

A number of elements in this story give us insight into teaching for commitment. The most obvious is what happens as a result of the teaching: Paul alters his *behavior* relationship to his stepchildren. Rather than staying angry and frustrated with them, he decides to do something—to get into counseling. Where does this decision come from? It is closely related to Paul's insight into his own past. He began to remember things about his father's style of parenting. This remembering took place in the midst of a fairly honest and deep level of sharing involving some risk on Paul's part. It led to a process of reflection. Paul began to stand back from his present style of parenting and evaluate whether or not it was an adequate way of relating to his stepchildren. An important part of this reflection involved considering what Christian parenting is all about and how his inherited model measured up to the theological understanding of parenting he was beginning to form.

All these factors working together led Paul to make a decision to do something about his style of parenting. All of them are important aspects of teaching for commitment. For the moment, it is enough to form a general idea of what this kind of teaching is all about. In my view, the heart of teaching for commitment involves inviting people to reinterpret some part of their life story in a way that alters their commitment in a specific area of their life.

This reinterpretation is done in relation to some part of the Christian story. In Paul's case, he was asked to consider new ways of thinking about Christian parenting, providing him a vantage point from which to look at his relationship with his stepchildren. Briefly put, we might say that teaching for commitment involves helping people reinterpret part of their life story in light of the Christian story in such a manner that some area of their life is changed. Probably, the key to understanding what this kind of teaching is all about is grasping the important role that story plays in shaping people's understandings of their lives.

Narrative as the Shape of Personal Identity

In chapter 2, we saw that it is probably not adequate to think of commitment primarily as a matter of human will. Inviting our students to use their willpower to become more dedicated in their relationship to God is likely to be ineffective. This is because the human will is grounded in something deeper: the underlying story by which humans make sense of their lives. It is this story—what we will call *personal identity narrative*—that influences the various decisions and choices people make.

This is not to say people have no freedom to use their wills. Of course they do. It is to say, however, that the fundamental direction of their wills is strongly influenced by the underlying narrative they use to understand themselves. It is this story that leads them to see certain things as choices in the first place and provides them with models to carry out the choices they make.

We can see this in the very different responses that

two people make to the same set of circumstances. Imagine the following situation. An upper level executive makes improper sexual advances to two of the secretaries in his office. One woman, who has been with the company for fifteen years, is totally paralyzed by his overtures. For her entire life, she has viewed herself as standing in a subordinate relationship to men, especially male authority figures. She sees herself as the kind of woman who is always ready and willing to put her own needs aside to help her husband, her children, and her boss.

Now, however, she is confronted with a situation in which this understanding of herself does not seem to work. She cannot be true to her personal moral principles and her boss's overtures. The only choice she sees is to quit her job. The story by which she understands herself presents her with no alternative. She cannot imagine acting in a nondependent or confrontive manner.

In sharp contrast, her co-worker sees a different set of options. Raised in a family of strong women who had no difficulty acting as equals with men in the home, this woman is used to seeing men and women fight and is not afraid of expressing her own needs and rights. Much younger than her co-worker she sees herself as "on the way up," viewing the secretarial job as a temporary stopping point on the way to a more satisfying career. It is a way of making money in order to go back to college.

Her boss's advances throw this woman off guard temporarily, and then they make her extremely angry. She does not want to quit her job. It pays well and is located near her apartment. As she thinks about how to respond, she sees a number of options: She can quit and make a big stink; she can confront her boss and see how he responds; or she can lay low and see if the advances cease when it becomes clear she is not going to respond. She also decides to see a lawyer and to begin keeping records of her boss's behavior toward her.

Obviously, this is an overly simplified scenario. Much more would need to be said to gain a good understanding of the stories that lie behind these two women's different responses. The important point to be made, however, involves the different way each woman frames the situation and the choices she sees herself as having. These different responses are not a simple matter of the will: deciding to choose this course of action or that. Rather, the very choices each woman sees herself as having are strongly influenced by the underlying story she uses to understand herself as an actor in the situation. The scenario invites us to ask several questions: What is meant by story or narrative? How does it relate to personal identity?

Most of us know intuitively what a story is. We have heard stories since we were children. As adults, many of us like to read books that weave good stories. A story or narrative is a type of literature that creates a plot, involving several characters, that unfolds through time. The plot of a narrative is composed of the various events which the author weaves together to provide a description of the action as it progresses. Of special importance to the plot are the critical incidents which mark the turning points of the story. These tell us crucial facts about the characters and move the story along.

In recent years, many scholars have pointed out that narrative is not only a particular type of literature but also a useful way to understand how humans make sense of their lives.[1] As one author has put it, narrative is the shape of personal identity.[2] What does this mean?

The concept "identity" refers to those qualities of a person or object that persist through time. The identity of an oak tree, for example, is that which makes the tree an oak over the course of its life, from the time it is a tiny seedling to the time it becomes a towering tree. If the tree is cut down and burned in a fire, it loses its identity as an oak as it is transformed into ashes.

When applied to humans, identity refers to those qualities of a person that persist through time, providing continuity at each stage of life. It is often easy to look at the old class picture of a friend and pick out his or her face amid all the children in the class. Certain characteristics have persisted over time in spite of the many, obvious changes: the eyes have remained the same; the face is still round.

Personal identity refers to the way that each of us understands our own identity: This is how I see myself over the course of my life. This is who I am and how I have come to be this way. While we all depend on the way that others see us and relate to us, personal identity refers to the way we see ourselves.

Narrative is the shape of personal identity. We know ourselves through our stories. This is because personal identity is an attempt to make sense of the history of our lives: how we have become who we are over time. In understanding who we are—forming a sense of personal identity—we weave together the important events and characters of our life into a meaningful plot unfolding through time. In short, our self-understanding naturally takes a narrative form.

Teaching for Commitment as the Reinterpretation
of Life Stories

We address the personal identity narrative when we are teaching for commitment. This is because personal identity is the well-spring of the larger and smaller commitments of our students. Personal identity exerts a powerful influence on the ways people invest their time and energy. It lies behind the relationships they enter into or avoid, the personal style they use at work or at home, and the kind of lifestyle they hope to achieve. This is why attempts to elicit a faith commitment from our students solely by appealing to their wills does not go deep enough. Their wills are directed by the narratives that shape their personal identities.

We as teachers need to realize that our students' composition of their personal identity narratives is never a finished process. The underlying stories by which people understand themselves change over the course of their lives. How does this take place?

The act of creating a story, any story, is always selective. It involves focusing on some events and relationships and leaving others out. This process of selection is based on what I will call *interpretive keys*.[3] These are the key events, incidents, or relationships that provide the guiding pattern for an author's interpretation of the story as a whole.

We see this at work in the Gospels' descriptions of Jesus. These narratives are selective in what they tell us about Jesus. Many details are left out: the kind of food Jesus ate, how long his hair was, how much sleep he got at night. Only significant events and relationships are selected for inclusion. The plot, moreover, is guided by a dominant interpretive key—the Passion, Jesus' suffering and death on the cross—that is used to interpret the meaning of the whole of Jesus' life and work. Even the account of Jesus' birth, for example, is portrayed as foreshadowing the suffering that is to come. His family is forced to flee to Egypt, and the innocent babies of Bethlehem are slaughtered.

Likewise, interpretive keys help us shape our personal identity narratives. A man who views himself as insecure and an underachiever, for example, might point to his relationship with an older brother as a crucial factor in shaping his self-understanding. His brother excelled in athletics and school without even trying, while he had to struggle hard just to earn average grades and to make a sports team. Very early on, he internalized a sense that he did not quite measure up, something he felt was played out in his high school and college years. An interpretive process is at work here in which one important relationship is used to interpret the meaning of this man's personal history.

Change in personal identity takes place primarily when important alterations occur in the interpretive keys which people use to guide their stories. Most of us have experienced this ourselves as we moved from one stage of life to another. Parents who were seen as too restrictive and protective during teenage years, for example, suddenly may be viewed as prudent and tough-minded when our own children reach adolescence.

In the same way, the man described above might come to realize at a later point in his life that he learned to compensate for his feelings of not measuring up by working harder than others and being well-organized. He might come to realize that these characteristics

helped him achieve career goals that far surpassed those
of his older brother, who never was able to get beyond
seeing high school as the best years of his life. He might
even come to appreciate having grown up in his brother's
shadow, for it was there that he learned the values of
self-reliance and perseverance. New interpretive keys
would have led to a new understanding of his history and,
ultimately, to a new personal identity narrative.

The central task in teaching for commitment is to
provide our students with the opportunity to begin to
reinterpret the stories by which they form their personal
identities. This is done by helping them discern new and
more adequate interpretive keys to guide the way they
view themselves and their life-commitments. Where do
these new interpretive keys come from? From our students' own experience? From the world around them?

From a Christian perspective, neither of these is fully
adequate. Our task as teachers is to help students discover the interpretive keys to their personal identity
narratives in the story of Jesus Christ. Teaching commitment, thus, is primarily a matter of bringing together in
a meaningful way the story of scripture that describes
God's dealings with the world and culminates in Jesus
Christ, and the life stories of our students.

Teaching as Invitation

It is helpful, I believe, to think of teaching that focuses
on commitment as a form of invitation. The primary goal
of teaching for commitment is to invite people to receive
the gift of a new story. As they do so, the larger and
smaller commitments making up the pattern of their lives
will gradually begin to be reshaped. Thinking of teaching

as a matter of invitation is important, because it stands in sharp contrast to the kind of psychological pressure that sometimes is identified with teaching commitment.

As we invite our students to form new commitments, we would do well to keep in mind Jesus' parable of the great banquet found in Luke 14:15–24. In the parable, the host decides to give a great feast. He invites various guests and, then, oversees the cooking of the food, the preparation of the table, and the notification of the guests when the banquet is ready. He does not force them to accept his invitation, however. When the invited guests give excuses, he sends his servants elsewhere to invite others who are eager to accept.

So it is in teaching for commitment. Just as the man prepared a sumptuous banquet, our task is to prepare a teaching plan that is as thoughtful and as creative as possible. We cannot force students to change, however, any more than the host could force his invited guests to come. Our task is to extend the invitation. Then we must trust in the mysterious workings of God's Spirit.

Planning to Teach for Commitment: A Three-Step Process

In preparing to teach for commitment, it often is helpful to move through three steps in our planning: (1) choose the area of commitment that is the focus of our teaching; (2) decide on the basic pattern that our teaching will take, a pattern which should include five different aspects of commitment; and (3) create or find learning activities that can be used in each of the different parts of our teaching. Each of these steps will make more sense as they are described in greater detail below.

Once more, these steps do not represent a planning process that every teacher ought to move through in lockstep fashion. Rather, they point to important areas that need to be considered in our preparation. Teaching for commitment is a highly creative activity, and we can expect this creativity to be reflected in our planning. Each teacher should feel free to adapt this process to his or her own style and gifts.

Step One: Deciding What to Teach

The first step focuses on choosing the area of commitment we want our teaching to emphasize. Throughout this chapter, the phrase "area of commitment" will refer to the subject we have decided to teach. This might involve something as fundamental as our students' personal commitment to Christ or might focus more narrowly on one sphere of their life: family, work, politics, or church. Whether the focus is narrow or broad, our task is to help students consider how their commitment in this area is grounded in their personal identity narrative and to open up a process of reinterpretation in light of some part of the Christian story.

This means it is crucial we choose a topic that has important, personal significance to the group we are teaching. We are going beyond transmitting information and leading a good discussion. We are inviting our students to change their lives. In the first stages of planning we need to think through why this topic or area should be studied by this particular group. It is helpful if the topic is something they are interested in and want to deal with themselves.

Many programs in the church grow out of the felt

needs of its members or those people in the community the church is trying to reach. The church leaders or teachers systematically and intentionally try to identify areas certain groups in the church are struggling with and would like the teaching ministry to address: parenting, planning for retirement, singles and sexuality, taking care of older parents, peacemaking, life after divorce, and coping with teens, to list but a few examples.

When we are teaching a class on an ongoing basis, we can give the class a chance to identify the needs and interests they would like to have addressed when the time comes to plan for the coming year. The needs and interests identified are prime candidates for topics that can be taught using the approach described in this chapter. People are struggling with their commitments in these areas already. Our job is to help them deepen this struggle through memory and reflection and to help them begin to understand it in light of the Christian story. This is what teaching for commitment is all about.

This sort of "needs-based" planning, however, does not go far enough. It often leaves untouched precisely those areas that people need to struggle with most. If we take the reality of sin seriously, then we cannot assume our students will automatically recognize what they really need. In our planning we must try to view our students in light of the "needs" that the gospel reveals. Sometimes these areas are sure to meet resistance.

It may well be, for example, that the baby boomers who are returning to the church during midlife need to struggle as much with issues of materialism and careerism as the areas of intimacy and personal meaning they seem to prefer.[4] Often, only in the light of the gospel can our real and deeper needs be seen. As we plan to teach, we must enter into a process of spiritual discernment in which we attempt to identify those areas of commitment our students need to face. We should invite the class, the minister, or appropriate committees to enter into this process of discernment with us.

Step Two: Projecting a Larger Pattern

The second step is to determine the larger pattern that will guide our teaching. It might be helpful to think of this pattern as composed of five basic parts: remembering, reflecting, encountering, sharing, and deciding. While these will be described in greater detail below, it might be helpful to say a few words about each part at this point.

- Remembering: Inviting students to recollect important parts of their life stories in relation to the focus of our teaching;
- Reflecting: Inviting students to stand back from their lives to discern important patterns or themes;
- Encountering: Inviting students to engage some aspect of the Christian story, especially as it is brought into focus in Jesus Christ.
- Sharing: Inviting students to disclose parts of their story usually kept hidden from others.
- Deciding: Inviting them to make decisions about how they will live their lives differently in light of new understandings of who they are.

It is not difficult to see each of these aspects at work in important persons in the Bible. Moses, for example, *encounters* God at several points in his life. When God speaks to him through the burning bush, he is forced to *remember* his past in Egypt and the reason he fled into the wilderness. He *reflects* upon his difficulties as a speaker and offers this to God as an excuse. In spite of his grave reservations, he *decides* to accept the commission God is placing upon him and *shares* this news with Jethro and Aaron. The triumphant climax of the whole sequence of events set in motion by this encounter is *remembered* later in the Song of Moses found in Exodus 15. Throughout scripture, we see example after example of periods of remembering, reflecting, encountering, sharing, and deciding as part of a new commitment in the life of faith.

Think of Paul. He too had a dramatic encounter with God that led him into a period of reflection. We constantly find him remembering his past in his letters and sharing his insights with others. Time after time, he decides to undertake some work on behalf of the Lord. Once again, each of the five aspects of commitment can be found. Paul's encounter with Christ leads him to reinterpret his life story through a new set of interpretive keys, altering his commitments radically. He is no longer Saul the Pharisee, persecuting the Christians, but Paul the apostle, leader of a missionary faith.

These five aspects are the focus of our teaching when we address the commitment side of the faith cube. As we plan to teach commitment, it is extremely important that we do not view these aspects as steps that should be moved through in the order given above: first, remembering; then, reflecting, and so on. Rather, these five aspects are like pieces of colored glass that can be put together in a wide variety of ways to form different patterns. Our task as teachers is to create the pattern by which the parts fit together. Following a brief description of the third step, more will be said about how we might determine this larger pattern.

Step Three: Planning Learning Activities

The third step in planning is finding or creating learning activities that can structure each part of the teaching pattern we have formed in the previous step. A learning activity is any intentional sequence of actions that the teacher uses to help students engage the subject matter. Examples of learning activities will be given as we examine in greater detail each of the five parts of teaching commitment listed in the previous step.

In our planning, if learning activities do not immediately come to mind, we would do well to talk to other teachers or consult books that describe different teaching methods. A bibliography of books that may prove helpful has been placed at the end of this book. In the learning activities described below, only enough information has been given to provide a general idea of what the activity involves. Our task in planning is to find those activities best suited to both our students and to the goals of our teaching.

Putting the Steps Together

Each part of this planning process is difficult in its own right. Identifying possible issues students feel they need to struggle with and discerning their deeper needs in light of the gospel (step 1) are not easy tasks. Setting up a basic pattern of teaching that integrates the five aspects (step 2) and finding appropriate learning activities for each aspect (step 3) also are demanding. One strategy that might be helpful in moving through each of these steps involves working with planning cards. Once we have chosen the general area of commitment that is the focus of our teaching, we need to decide how we are to deal with each of the five aspects of teaching commitment. We can do this for a single session or think in terms of several sessions if we are planning a retreat or a series. Working with index cards, we write on the top of five cards one of the five aspects of teaching commitment: remembering, reflecting, and so on. We then begin to consider what sort of learning activity we might like to use to facilitate each aspect.

On an index card for reflecting, for example, we might write down learning activities like "individuals work by themselves and write down two events from their life that have bearing on this topic" or "small groups reflect on this topic and come up with two insights to share with the larger group." Each time we come up with a different learning activity, it should be put on its own card, with the aspect it represents noted at the top. Likely, we will end up with more than one card for several of the aspects. Sharing, for example, might take place at several points in the session or retreat. Each time it takes place, a different index card is created.

The goal, of course, is to arrange these cards into the larger pattern of a session and/or series. Usually, we move back and forth in our planning between forming a larger pattern and deciding on specific learning activities. As activities occur to us, we might decide on a different pattern. Or we might decide to alter the pattern we initially projected, leading us to come up with new learning activities. This is the advantage of working with cards. They can be rearranged quite easily.

If we are teaching for commitment in a series or a retreat, it is important to assure a balance among the five aspects. Once we have done our planning, we can lay out the cards in proper order to see if we have achieved this. Do we have only a few activities that enable people to decide how they will change their commitments? Are remembering and sharing over-represented? Is encountering the Christian story left out of every session but one? If we do not find a balance among the five aspects, we may need to consider altering our overall plan. Each of the aspects represents an important part of the process by which persons decide to alter their commitments. Neglecting an aspect can potentially subvert the entire process.

Encouraging Our Students to Try This Approach

Clearly, a level of risk, reflection, and self-disclosure is required with this approach that is not always found in other teaching approaches. How can we invite our students to move with us to this level? Many times, we are asking them to do things they are not used to doing.

One idea is to start with a topic based on the felt needs of our students. If we are teaching an ongoing class, we might let them participate in the planning process in the manner described at an earlier point. If we are teaching a special, short-term series, we might invite several people who are likely to be interested in this series to meet with us and share their interests. As noted above, "needs-based" planning is not enough, but it is a good place to start with a group unaccustomed to the kind of teaching described in this chapter.

It is also good to give participants a general idea in advance of what they are getting into. That way if they want to opt out, they can do so. Conversely, those who decide to participate have a heightened sense that they have chosen to do so.

Since teaching for commitment involves a level of reflection and self-disclosure that goes beyond the norm of many classes, it is generally a good idea to start off with learning activities that are less threatening. We might move the group toward deeper levels of remembering and sharing, for example, only gradually. Likewise, we might consider ways of helping groups form that can stay together for an extended period of time, for the entire course of a series or retreat, for instance. We might be sure to give the participants the chance to choose their own groups. The goal of these techniques and others like them is to ease the participants into reflection, recollection, and honest sharing.

Perhaps most important of all, we should try to walk the fine line between respecting our students' right to refuse to go deeper in their remembering, sharing, or reflecting and giving them the chance to enter into an educational experience that is personally meaningful. Remember, our task in teaching for commitment is one of invitation, not coercion. This should not keep us, however, from being as creative and as compelling in our invitation as possible.

A Summary of the Planning Process

The three steps described above can be summarized as follows:

1. Choose the area of commitment that is the focus of your teaching.
   —Consider the needs and interests of the students.
   —Go beyond "needs-based" planning and discern areas

of commitment the Christian story presses the students
to consider.

2. Decide on the basic pattern your teaching will take,
a pattern that should include five aspects of commitment: remembering, reflecting, encountering, sharing,
deciding.

3. Create or find learning activities that can be used in
each of the different parts of your teaching.
   —Recall learning activities from your experiences as a
   student.
   —Talk to other teachers and read books to find useful
   learning activities.

The Five Aspects of Teaching for Commitment:
What Is at Stake?

We now have before us a general idea of the planning
involved in teaching for commitment. It is time to go
one step further and get a clearer idea of the five aspects
of teaching for commitment: remembering, reflecting,
encountering, sharing, and deciding. For the most part,
the rest of this chapter is devoted to describing each of
these aspects and providing examples of learning activities that can be used to teach them.

As we zero in on each aspect, we should keep in mind
the overall goal of our teaching. By themselves, remembering, reflecting, encountering, sharing, and deciding
can be used in a wide variety of teaching approaches. It
is the way they work together that enables them to
create a context in which our students examine their
faith commitments. When we are addressing the commitment side of the faith cube, we are inviting our
students to deepen their devotion and dedication to
God in a particular area of their lives. This involves

inviting them to reinterpret their life story as it relates to this area in light of their encounter with the Christian story.

Remembering

Augustine, the great Christian theologian of the fifth century, wrote in his *Confessions*: "Look into my heart, O Lord, for it was your will that I should remember these things and confess them to you."[5] Making use of memory is the task of this aspect of teaching commitment: remembering so we might bring the past into the healing and transforming presence of God.

Why is it important for us as individuals to remember? Because our lives are shaped in powerful ways by our memories of the past. Personal identity is based on memory. From the many events and relationships making up our histories, we remember those that seem to help us make sense of who we are, where we have come from, and where we are going. This memory-based sense of who we are determines the pattern of commitments we make in our lives.

One of our most important tasks as teachers is to enable people to become aware of the story lying behind the commitments they have made in the area being studied in class.[6] Often this is a story that is not operating at a conscious level.

I recall a man who literally turned pale with shock during an educational event on racism as he began to recall the kinds of racial stereotypes he had encountered as a child. For the first time in years, he remembered the way his maid always referred to him as "Sir," even though he was just a boy. He remembered swirling firecrackers that were called "nigger-chasers." It was only through a process of remembering his own story that this person began to become aware of the ways these racist images were still at work in his life as an adult. He could not immediately cast off his racism, but he had taken an important first step: remembering.

Learning Activities

Sometimes remembering is a painful, wrenching process. It is not possible for us, as teachers, to force our students to confront the past. Rather, our approach must be one of invitation. What we can do, however, is choose the kinds of learning activities that are most likely to work for our particular group of students. It may be helpful for us to think in terms of two different types of learning activities that can be used to help people remember: *focused remembering* and *meditative remembering*.

Learning activities that fall under the first type do not move beyond the kind of remembering that is accessible to us in our everyday lives. In focused remembering, we ask our students to look into the past in a focused, reflective, and searching manner. In meditative remembering, by contrast, we invite them to draw on creative dimensions of their selves not used frequently in our scientific, rational society. Memories accessible through dreams, creative expression, and meditative states are explored.

Examples of learning activities used for each of these types of remembering are offered below. In creating or finding a learning activity to use in our teaching, we must judge what type of activity is appropriate for our

particular group. Some groups will not tolerate meditative remembering, especially in its more creative forms.
Much depends on what the group has experienced in the
past and how much it trusts us as teachers. We should
not sell our people short, however. In teaching, as in
life, the old proverb holds: "Nothing ventured, nothing
gained." Unless we are willing to take some risks, our
students might not get the chance to tap inner resources
they desperately need to draw on.

Focused Remembering

Life chapters. In this learning activity, students are
invited to pretend they have been asked to write an
autobiography of their lives.[7] The publisher has asked
them for the table of contents in which they list the title
of each chapter. They work on these individually and
then write them on newsprint to share with others.

Image-of-God exercise. This learning activity invites
students to look at how their image of God has changed
over the course of their lives.[8] They are asked to draw
four boxes of equal size on the right side of a piece of
paper. Next to the first box, they write "My childhood
image of God." Next to the second, they write, "My
adolescent image of God"; next to the third, "My adult
image of God"; and next to the fourth, "My present
image of God." They may draw in additional boxes if
they are older. Students are then asked to remember
their image of God at each of these points in their lives
and to write down a word or phrase or draw a picture
representing their image in each box.

Learning to pray. This learning activity is designed to help people remember where their understandings of prayer came from. Students are asked to form three columns under three headings, moving from left to right: Prayer Teachers/How They Prayed/What I Learned. In the first column, they list people who have contributed in some way to their understanding of prayer: parents, church school teachers, grandparents, a minister, a youth leader, a college roommate, the author of a book on prayer, a retreat leader, or a television personality. In the second column, they are asked to remember how these people prayed: in an informal conversational style, using set prayers at supper or bedtime, in a highly emotional way or with formality. Under the third column, they are asked to jot down what they learned from this person about how to pray.

Meditative Remembering

Guided Imagery. This learning activity can open up memories and foster insights of a highly significant nature. The first step involves inviting our students to go through a series of relaxation exercises that move them into a meditative state. Focusing on their breathing and tensing/relaxing one muscle group at a time are helpful.

The second step involves the use of guided imagery. We invite them to allow their imagination to form the images that are suggested, images that involve some part of their past. These can take many forms. We might invite them to remember their childhood bedroom, for example. We might ask them to look over the various parts of the room. Are favorite objects present? What do they see when they look out the window? How does the room "feel"? Does it make them feel safe or troubled? Happy or sad? We might invite them to focus on a family member. When they were children, what did this person look like? What feelings did they have toward that person?

A variant of guided imagery that involves even more creativity is to help students create a scene in their imaginations that is open-ended, allowing them to be more active participants in the creation of the imagery. For instance, we might invite them into a special art museum which allows persons to peer into the past. They enter a room with their name on it and see large blank screens on each of the three walls. They will go to each screen in succession and see a different picture taking shape. The screen on the first wall forms a picture representing their childhood. The second screen represents adolescence, and the third, young adulthood. At the end of each guided meditation, we should invite people to come back gradually to their normal consciousness.

If it does not seem possible to use this learning activity in the setting normally used by the class, we might consider providing the members of the class with a sheet that has the meditation written on it. They can then tape record the directions and play them back in the privacy of their home. They could share their memories and images in the next session.

Praying the Psalms with Feeling. This learning activity uses the Psalms to help students open up feelings hidden much of the time in church, especially feelings of anger, sadness, hatred, and joy.⁹ All students will need to read the psalm from the same translation. They are asked to read through it one time and identify the different feelings expressed. We then ask them to read the psalm aloud as a group, expressing as much feeling as possible. They should try to block out others and totally identify with the psalm. When it is sad, they are to be sad. When it is angry, they are to be angry. After the group has read the psalm aloud, the students are invited to close their eyes and enter into a period of silence. In the silence, they should allow words or phrases of the psalm to enter their minds. Then, they should allow images of times when they felt like the psalmist to come into their minds. They should not "force" these memories into awareness. These should surface spontaneously. It is all right if nothing comes.

Dream Journal. This learning activity works best as part of a teaching series in which the same group is together for a number of weeks. The group members should be encouraged to remember their dreams during the coming week, using the following technique. Before going to bed, they should place a pad of paper and pencil on their bedside table. When they wake up during the night or first thing in the morning, they should quickly jot down the dream they were having. We might ask them to look over the dreams they have remembered before the next session and choose the dream most related to the subject studied by the class. In the next class, they will have a chance to share it with others.

Reflecting

This aspect of teaching commitment invites students to stand back from the memories they have surfaced and see if they can discern a pattern or significant themes. There are three basic reasons why this is an important part of teaching commitment.

First, the expression of emotion must be linked with understanding if long-lasting change is to take place. Very often, remembering stirs up powerful feelings that are shared with the group. It might seem to be enough simply to express these feelings in a supportive group, leading to a release of dammed-up emotion. Research has indicated, however, that this does not go far enough.[10] Long-lasting change is far more likely to take place if the expression of feeling is accompanied by an understanding of the pattern of events or relationships which lie behind these feelings. The reflective aspect of teaching commitment is designed to help this occur.

A second important reason that reflection is important has to do with helping our students become aware of the "interpretive keys" lying at the heart of their personal identity narratives. Most of the time, we are not aware of the key events or relationships from the past that we use to interpret the whole. These are not obvious, either to ourselves or to others. Learning activities which invite reflection, however, can help people become aware of these keys, especially if these activities involve reflection over time with a supportive group and a competent leader.

The third reason that reflection is needed is the way it helps the individual make links between the past and the present. This is an especially important part of teaching for commitment. We are not interested in helping students surface memories just for the sake of remembering. Our ultimate goal is to help them begin to redirect their commitments in the present. Standing back and looking at important events and relationships from the past can help our students see the ways that the past continues to live on in the present.

Learning Activities

Each of these learning activities builds on one offered in the remembering section. As we have noted, however, reflecting need not follow remembering in teaching for commitment. In the appendix, we will explore a variety of patterns that can be used to structure our teaching. For the present, it makes sense to see how various learning activities fit together. Since we have described remembering already, we will build on it in this section.

Writing the Title of Your Life Story. Building on the Life Chapters exercise, this activity invites students to spend some time pondering the chapter headings they have written in order to come up with a title for their life story as a whole.[11] Often, it is helpful for them to write a brief paragraph describing why they chose this title. What does it say about how they view their life to this point? Are there key chapters in the story which lie behind their choice of the title?

This Is a Time in My Life When . . . This learning activity also builds on the Life Chapters exercise.[12] Students are invited to focus on the present chapter of their life story and write down their reflections. It usually is helpful for us to ask some prompting questions to guide their reflection. When did their present chapter begin: several months ago or several years ago? What were the marker events that initiated this chapter: a move, a divorce, a new relationship, an injury? What engages their attention and energy right now? How are things going in their significant relationships? What are their hopes and dreams right now? Their fears and worries? What is God to them at this time: close, distant, friend, stranger, enemy?

Image-of-God Reflections. This learning activity builds on the image-of-God exercise described in the previous section. In that exercise, students are asked to jot down phrases, words, or pictures that represent their images of God during childhood, adolescence, young adulthood, and the present. It is useful to follow this with a series of questions that help them reflect upon the changes and continuity in their images of God: What is the relationship between their childhood and adolescent images of God? Does their adolescent image build on their childhood image, reject it, or replace it with something new? What were the sources of their images during both of these periods? How has their understanding of God changed over the course of adulthood? How is this represented in the pictures/words/phrases on their sheet? Would they describe their religious life as one of continuity or discontinuity?

Guided Imagery Reflections. This learning activity builds on the guided imagery exercise described above. Reflection is especially important when we are using meditative remembering that can stir up highly emotional memories. We begin by asking our students to write down a brief description of the imagery that emerged as they experienced the meditation. If they were focusing on their childhood bedroom, for example, what sorts of things did they see, hear, smell, and feel? We then ask them to write down a paragraph or two about what the imagery is trying to say to them. Invite them to pretend that their memory is a friend who can only communicate with them indirectly through symbols and imagery. What is that friend trying to tell them? We should ask reflective questions that gradually move from the imagery in its concreteness to more abstract reflection. As they saw their childhood room, what was the one item that really stood out? What kinds of feelings do they associate with this item: happy, sad, anxious, or funny? What does this item tell them about the rest of their childhood? Does it stand out because it represents much of what their childhood was like or because it was so unusual? Does this item remind them of anyone in particular? What was their relationship with that person? In a final step, we ask them to reflect on the relation of the imagery to their life in the present. What is it "telling" them about the way they are living their life today? How does it relate to the area of commitment that is the focus of their learning in this educational event?

Encountering

One of the most important parts of teaching for commitment is inviting our students to encounter some portion of scripture or Christian tradition that addresses the area of commitment that is the focus of our teaching. One contemporary theologian describes the intersection of the Christian story and our personal identity narratives as being like a collision.[13] Two forces moving in different directions, suddenly run in to one another. According to this image, God's Word does not merely confirm us where we are but "collides" with our personal identity narratives, forcing us to redirect our various commitments.

I have chosen to use the term *encounter,* rather than collision, although I want to retain the strong sense of redirection that is implied by collision. The Christian life is not always a matter of two opposing forces running into one another. Sometimes, our teaching builds on the commitments that persons already have made.[14] The processes of formation by which personal identity narrative is shaped contribute to continuity in the Christian life. This is continuity, however, that must remain open to the continual inbreaking and redirecting of God's Word.

Learning Activities

The root meaning of encounter is to meet face to face. Encounter, above all else, is a meeting. It is a gathering of two or more parties to engage in conversation. Moreover, it is a meeting of a particular sort: It is a face-to-face meeting. It is not a long-distance conference call. Nor is it a communication by letter or memo. It is a personal conversation. The heart of teaching the encounter aspect is fostering a personal conversation between our students and some aspect of scripture or Christian tradition. This involves three basic elements, representing our teaching goals at this point.

First, it involves choosing the subject matter for our

students to encounter and presenting it to them in ways that address them personally. If encounter is meeting face to face, our first task is to decide what subject we want to invite to the meeting and introducing it to our students. Our second task is to bring about a conversation between our students and the voice of scripture or tradition. This means facilitating the give and take of genuine conversation. Our third task is to help our students discover the way they have been affected personally by this conversation. What sort of new connections have they begun to discover between their lives and scripture or tradition? What new images or concepts have they gained by which to rethink their commitment in the area under study?

Paraphrasing Scripture. This learning activity invites students to look at a passage of scripture closely and to begin the task of relating it to their own lives.[15] The teacher starts by noting the difference between a literal translation and a paraphrase. The former keeps close to the original meaning of the text; the latter is freer in using modern words and concepts to affect today's audience in a manner that is comparable to the passage's original impact. Students are asked to paraphrase an assigned passage of scripture, using words and phrases that make it clear what the text has to say to their lives today. With groups that are not familiar with this learning activity, it is helpful to begin by paraphrasing the first two or three verses of the passage and then to ask one or two people to share what they have written. This gives people who are struggling with the exercise some idea how others are approaching the passage.

Candle, Arrow, Star, and Question Mark. In this activity, our students are asked to read through an assigned passage, marking the margins with symbols that indicate how certain verses strike them. I have seen different symbols used and have found the following particularly useful. An arrow is drawn when a verse or phrase strikes the readers as important. A candle or flame is drawn when a verse sparks an insight about their own life or the contemporary world. A star is drawn when a verse seems so important that they think they should memorize it. A question mark is used to indicate that they did not understand the verse or that it raises an important question. After a specified period of time, the group is called together and sharing begins, usually focusing on one category at a time and then building toward a more general discussion. When using this learning activity and the previous one, it is important for the teacher to encourage people to feel free to engage scripture with questions and personal insights. Sometimes they are reluctant to do so.

Being Parabled. This learning activity is especially useful as part of a retreat setting that has included periods of remembering and reflection at earlier points.[16] It begins with a brief period of discussion of parables in which they are described as stories based on a relatively commonplace situation that suddenly reverse the hearers' normal expectations and challenge them to look at something in a new way. This is followed by an examination of several of Jesus' parables that illustrate this reversal. Each person is then asked to write his or her own parable as it pertains to the area of commitment being studied. It is to be a relatively short story that embodies the kind of reversal that is found in the parables of Jesus. The session ends with the group gathering together and giving people the chance to share their parables with the entire group. If the group is large, the number who share should be limited. There are to be no comments by the author or the group after the parable is read. Each parable is simply received as a gift.

Sharing

This aspect of teaching commitment emerges naturally out of the others already described, and to a certain extent, it is artificial to separate it too sharply from the others. The key to this aspect is creating the possibility of *self-disclosure*. In chapter 4, we saw that there are four levels of communication: informal chit-chat, sharing of information, sharing of personal insights and feelings, and self-disclosure. During the sharing aspect of teaching commitment, we are striving to reach the fourth level. Our job is to foster a climate and to offer learning activities through which self-disclosure can take place.

To disclose means to unveil or reveal. Self-disclosure is the act of unveiling parts of ourself and revealing them to others. Research indicates that one of the most important factors in fostering self-disclosure is whether or not others are perceived as willing to share at the same level.[17] If we share something personal with a friend, for example, and he or she never shares at the same level, chances are good we will feel rebuffed and hold back from this sort of self-disclosure in the future.

As we plan for periods of sharing, then we must try to use learning activities that promote *mutual sharing*. We should try to encourage everyone to share. This means allowing enough time for this to take place. It also means we might need to break our group into small sharing groups. In general, it is less threatening to share with two or three people than with a larger group.

Other factors also promote the possibility of self-disclosure: *confidentiality* and the experience of *empathy*. Few of us are willing to share with others unless we believe they will maintain confidentiality. If you have ever disclosed something personal to a friend or a small group and then found out this personal information was shared with others, you know how hurt and angry this makes people. It is important, thus, to stress to the group that confidentiality be maintained.

Empathy is the capacity to enter into another person's perspective, especially his or her feelings. Empathy is far more important than giving advice when creating a climate for self-disclosure. When someone shares something important, especially if it involves struggle or pain, our natural inclination is to offer advice as a way of trying to provide help. While advice is appropriate at points, it can be a hindrance if it becomes the normal way a group or some of its members respond to self-disclosure. This is because advice deals with practical solutions, while self-disclosure focuses on the moment of self-discovery and self-expression. Rushing to quick solutions through advice-giving robs the sharer of the chance to struggle to put into words feelings and insights that he or she is just discovering. It's like a doctor offering a prescription before he or she knows what the illness is. It is far more important that the listeners empathize with the sharer.

We can do several simple things to promote empathy during periods of sharing. First, we can directly ask people to refrain from giving advice: "This is not the time to tell persons what they ought to do. This is the time to listen, trying to get inside their way of seeing things." Second, we can help give them instructions as to how they can listen empathetically: "Listen especially for the feelings that are shared. What comes through?" or "Pay attention to your own feelings and insights as the other person shares. Perhaps, they will give you clues about what is going on." Third, we can invite the listeners to offer to the sharer what they are hearing and experiencing in a tentative, open-ended fashion. This leaves the sharer free to accept or reject what is said.

Learning Activities

Sharing Groups. This learning activity is probably the one used most frequently to facilitate sharing. It sometimes is referred to as buzz groups or subgroups. It involves groups of three to six people which are formed when the class as a whole is too large for meaningful self-disclosure to take place. It is very important that the leader give clear instructions to the sharing groups when they break off from the total group, stating exactly what they are to do. It is probably best if these are written on the blackboard or a piece of paper given to each group in addition to being given verbally. We should also be sure to include the approximate length of time each group will have. It may also be appropriate to appoint a timekeeper and a facilitator in each group. This gets the group started more quickly and ensures that each person has a chance to share.

Circle Response. This learning activity gets everyone involved individually and then opens the discussion to the entire group.[18] The group is seated in a circle. The leader or facilitator begins by asking a question that focuses on the area of commitment being studied, pausing to give the group time to think. He or she then asks the person on the left to respond to the question, moving to the next person when the first response is completed. Moving from person to person around the circle, each person is given a chance to share. No comments are made by others until the entire circle has been completed. The leader then invites the group members to ask one another questions that arose as sharing took place around the circle. People are given a chance to respond. The leader gradually moves the group to an open-ended discussion.

Concentric Circles. In this learning activity, several people move their chairs inside a circle composed of the rest of the group. Hence, it is sometimes called "The Fish Bowl Exercise." The people on the inside of the circle discuss some facet of the area of commitment being studied. The others on the outside listen to what is said without asking questions or making comments. Sometimes they are asked to listen for specific words, issues, or feelings. After a certain period of time, the conversation ends, and the leader invites the members of the outside circle to reflect on what they heard. After an initial round of sharing, others may move to the center of the circle to discuss a slightly different aspect of commitment. A similar process of discussion then follows.

Deciding

The deciding aspect comes the closest to what most people have in mind when they think of teaching for commitment, since it involves elements of human will and choice. As I am using it here, however, deciding is only one part of a larger process, a process in which people have come to a deeper understanding of their personal identity narrative through remembering, reflecting, encountering, and sharing. In light of the insights that have been gained, they are now given a chance to make a decision about how they are going to redirect their commitments.

This is a crucial moment in teaching for commitment. It attempts to help people move beyond the classroom or the retreat center to their everyday lives. It is both a culmination and an intensification of everything that has gone before. It is a culmination in the sense that we now ask people to pull together the learnings they have gained to that point. It is an intensification in the sense that we now invite people to confront the hard realities of change. The time of decision is at hand! How are they going to live their lives differently? How are they going to redirect their commitments?

There are three basic parts of this time of decision. First, we must provide people with the opportunity to pull together all that they have learned at other points in their remembering, reflecting, encountering, and sharing. Typically, this should involve *self-expression* on their part. They should be invited to summarize their learnings in words, images, pictures, writing, or in some other form of expression.

Second, we need to invite people to face the "*So*

what?" question. In light of their new insights, what should be different about their faith commitments? Third, we should invite people to discern the *concrete steps* that need to be taken to bring about real change in their lives. The key word here is *concrete.* We want to help people focus on what they can do tomorrow or next week. We should encourage them to be specific. One small step actually taken is better than a huge, risky leap never made. There is much truth in the saying, "The road to hell is paved with good intentions." If they are willing to take some risky steps, encourage them to think through concretely how they can do so.

Learning Activities

Writing Our Life's Next Chapter. This learning activity builds on the kind of remembering and reflecting already described.[19] People are asked to write two scenarios, both of which describe their lives five years from the present. In the first scenario, they describe their life as if their hopes and dreams were fulfilled. In the second, they describe their life as if their worries and fears were realized. The group members are then asked to put the two scenarios side by side and to search for the factors that will make a difference. They should ask: Which factors are beyond my control? Which factors can I do something about? People then are broken into sharing groups with three or four members. Each person shares the two scenarios with the group and asks the group members what they think will make the difference. Only after the group shares, does each individual divulge the factors he or she identified. After each person has had a chance to share, the group spends time helping each member discern one or two concrete steps that can be taken in the near future to move toward the fulfillment of the positive scenario.

Personal Application in Bible Study. Bible study that invites people to an altered commitment cannot avoid moments of personal decision. The participants must decide how they are going to live their lives differently in light of their study of scripture. This involves two basic questions which will be framed differently in light of the biblical material being studied. First, can you summarize what this passage has been saying to you about how you should live your life? Second, are there one or two ways you can live differently in the coming week in light of your insights? The group should be told that it will have a chance to share how things went during the next meeting.

Personal Testimony. This learning activity does not fulfill all three parts of the deciding aspect. It focuses primarily on the first part, giving expression to culminating insights. The gist of it is providing people with the opportunity to stand before the entire group and share the significant things they have learned and the changes they see ahead. For example, in an all-church retreat that has focused on the issue of world hunger, each family might be given the opportunity to make a small banner that symbolizes its commitment to an altered lifestyle. As the families gather for closing worship, each could be given the chance to share what they have made and the commitment it represents. Somewhat differently, the end of a series on Christian parenting might provide each parent or couple with the opportunity to list three or four significant insights on newsprint. Each parent or couple might then be given the chance to share one thing about their parenting they hope to change as a result of the class and why this item is important.

A Summary

 1. Remembering:
    —Invite, do not force people to remember, especially if this involves areas that are painful.
    —Use one of two types of learning activities:
      (1) Focused remembering
      (2) Meditative remembering
 2. Reflecting:
    —The expression of emotion is not enough. Use learning activities linking emotional expression and intellectual understanding.
    —Helping persons become aware of the interpretive keys of their personal identity narrative is an important part of altering their commitments.
    —Links between the past and the present are an important step in helping people see the ways that their present commitments are grounded in a deeper and longer story stretching into the past.
 3. Encountering:
    —Choose that portion of scripture or Christian tradition to be encountered and decide how its voice can address the students.
    —Facilitate a genuine dialogue between the students and the voice of scripture or tradition.
    —Help students discover and consolidate personal insights that have emerged from this conversation.

4. Sharing:
   —Provide everyone with the chance to share. Try to help mutuality to develop among students.
   —Strongly emphasize confidentiality. What is shared should stay in the group.
   —Encourage empathetic listening and responding by discouraging advice-giving and by instructing the class in how to listen.
5. Deciding:
   —Give people a chance to pull together and express their insights.
   —Invite them to struggle with the "So what?" question, helping them discern the changes that should take place in their lives.
   —Help them plan concrete steps that put in motion a process of change in their lives.

As has been emphasized repeatedly, one of the most important and difficult steps in the planning process is deciding how to fit together remembering, reflecting, encountering, sharing, and deciding into a larger pattern. These aspects can be put together in a variety of ways. Much of our decision will be governed by things like the kind of time we have available (an entire weekend, forty-five minutes), the format (retreat, series, ongoing class), and the learners (ages, preferred style of learning, cognitive stage). In the Appendix, I have outlined two different patterns using similar learning activities in order to illustrate the various ways the aspects of teaching commitment can be put together.

6

Teaching for Mystery:
The Role of Paradox
in Teaching

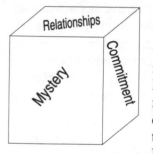

We conclude this study on teaching by focusing on the mystery side of the faith cube. A mystery is something secret or hidden. In theology, it refers to matters beyond human knowledge and comprehension. Mystery is an important part of faith. It is an acknowledgement of the fact that God cannot be comprehended fully by human understanding. God remains "other." As one of the great creeds of the early church puts it, God is "incomprehensible."[1] God's ways are not our ways. There are limits on our ability to understand God. The apostle Paul once wrote, "For now we see in a mirror, dimly, but then we will see face to face" (1 Cor. 13:12). An acknowledgement of mystery in faith is an acceptance of the fact that in this world we see dimly. Our ability to understand the incomprehensible God is limited.

Mystery and the Limits of Faith

Why is it important to acknowledge mystery as a dimension of faith? Over the course of human history, we see one attempt after another to press beyond the limits that are part of humanity's relationship with God. Things are said or done on God's behalf that reflect human interests and needs more than God's will. In the name of God, things are done that serve only the interests of the state, political party, church, or individual. The boundaries separating the sovereign, holy God and a sinful, self-deceptive humanity are collapsed.

An acknowledgement of the dimension of mystery in faith helps us accept the limits that are a part of our relationship with God. God remains other. We must not confuse our personal needs, our cultural biases, or our class prejudices with the ways of the Creator of heaven and earth. Whenever we do so, we are constructing a likeness of God that is really made in our own image. The prophet Isaiah warns us against this:

> To whom then will you liken God,
> or what likeness compare with him?
> . . . .
> It is he who sits above the circle of the earth,
> and its inhabitants are like grasshoppers.
> (Isa. 40:18,22)

Ultimately, God is beyond the likenesses we construct. Accepting this means acknowledging that mystery is part of faith. Certain boundaries must be respected in our relationship with God. Because of these boundaries, it is important to acknowledge that our understanding of God is limited, that is, finite, human, and much of the time, self-serving.

Teaching for mystery attempts to create a context in which students can come to terms with the limits that are part of their faith. It challenges them to become aware of the ways their current understanding of God is too small. This can be a painful and threatening process. None of us enjoy discovering that ideas we have cherished are not adequate or even are false.

Many of us can remember how painful it was to learn that Santa Claus does not exist. Likewise, we can remember how unsettling it was to discover that our parents are only human and not the ideal persons we had thought. Some of us experienced this same sort of disillusionment when we took a leadership position in our congregation for the first time and were exposed to the bickering and political maneuvering that sometimes characterizes church life. Likewise, many of us during the first years of marriage passed through a period when we shed the romantic notions of love that we brought to the marriage and began to realize that it is hard work for two different people to live together and to care for each other.

Each of these experiences of disillusionment is painful. People do not easily give up ideas that are important to them. Yet this process lies at the heart of teaching for mystery. It is an attempt to create a context in which people can come to terms with the limits of their present understanding of God. I have seen many seminary students pass through times of struggle and doubt, sometimes involving severe depression, as they began to realize that their views of the Bible, the minister's role, or the saving work of Christ could not pass the test of scholarly reflection. They were confronting firsthand the limits of their current understanding of God.

This is the heart of teaching for mystery. It is an attempt to help our students accept the limits that are part of faith. We gain important clues about how this sort of teaching takes place by examining the teaching of Jesus.

Parabolic Teaching

When we look at Jesus' teaching, one of the first characteristics that stands out is his use of parables. Much of the time, we think of Jesus' parables along the lines of a good sermon illustration.[2] We view him as taking an incident from everyday life and using it to simplify complex theological ideas for his audience. If we look more closely, however, we see that this is not what happened. Many times Jesus' disciples (much less the crowds) were confused by what he said in parables. They came to him later and asked for clarification. If parables are not simplified teaching stories, what are they?

A parable is a brief story, based on everyday life, that brings about a sudden reversal of the expectations of its hearers, opening them up to a new way of seeing God and the world in relation to God.[3] Far from being a simplified teaching illustration, a parable attempts to make strange what is normally taken for granted.[4] It does this through a sudden, unexpected reversal of the audience's expectations.

An excellent example of this sort of reversal is found in the parable of the Prodigal Son (Luke 15:11–32). As the story unfolds, we expect the self-indulgent, wasteful son to get what he deserves. After all, common sense tells us that fathers should reward dutiful sons, not those who squander their inheritance. Yet it is precisely this expectation the parable reverses. The father welcomes the prodigal son home and throws a great banquet in his honor. Understandably, the dutiful son is resentful.

This parable flies in the face of everything that makes sense in our normal way of looking at things. How can families and societies carry on if slothful and wasteful persons are rewarded and those who are dutiful neglected? Surely, there must be some hidden teaching in the parable that takes the realities of everyday life into account!

This is precisely what parables do not do, however. Their primary role is to open up and call into question our ordinary way of looking at things. Their sudden reversal of expectations overturns the logic of the world and invites us to look at God afresh. When a parable loses the capacity to generate a sense of surprise in its hearers, it ceases to function parabolically. Even the parables of Jesus can cease to function as parabolic teaching when they are integrated into our taken-for-granted assumptions about God. Teaching for mystery is focused on recapturing the sense of surprise and reversal at the heart of the parables. It invites us to acknowledge the limits of our understandings of God. To get a better idea how this is done, we must take a closer look at the role of paradox in the parables.

Paradox in Parabolic Teaching

Many biblical scholars have argued that paradox lies at the heart of Jesus' teaching in parables.[5] A paradox is a statement or an argument that seems self-contradictory when viewed from the perspective of common

sense.[6] In philosophy, it is sometimes described more
formally as two contrary propositions, both of which can
be established by sound arguments and affirmed as
true.[7] A paradox, thus, does not fit into the "logic" of
our normal way of looking at things. It creates contradictions in our taken-for-granted world, contradictions
which cannot be resolved as long as we hold to the
"logic" of our current frame of reference.[8]

To grasp the role of paradox in parabolic teaching, it
is important to understand how it is directed toward the
assumptions of those who are listening to the parable.
By contradicting one or more of the audience's assumptions, the entire "logic" of these assumptions is called
into question. The hearers are invited to shift to a new
frame of reference, a new way of understanding God
and themselves in relation to God.

We have seen something of this already in Jesus'
parable of the Prodigal Son. At a variety of levels, the
parable contradicts the assumptions of its audience:
dutiful sons are rewarded and slothful sons are pun-
ished; responsible fathers must use discipline to teach
responsible behavior to their children. When these assumptions are applied to God and to the religious life,
however, they become a problem. Or so Jesus seems to
imply in his teaching. His parable contradicts the
"logic" of these assumptions. This contradiction can
only be overcome by moving to a new frame of reference in which God's love is seen in all its extravagance
and not along the lines of reward-and-punishment
thinking used in everyday life.

Another well-known parable that illustrates the importance of paradox in parabolic teaching is the Good
Samaritan (Luke 10:29–37). Once more, it is important

to understand how the parable engages and, thereby, contradicts the assumptions of its audience. In the Good Samaritan, the very people whom Jesus' audience would have expected to do good—the priest and the Levite—do evil, walking by the badly beaten man. The person whom his audience would have expected to do evil—the Samaritan—turns out to be the source of good. Indeed, the Samaritan goes far beyond what reasonably could be expected in such a situation, bandaging the beaten man's wounds, interrupting his own journey to take the man to an inn, paying for the man's lodging, and promising to pay for additional expenses.

From our perspective today, it is easy to miss how shocking this parable would have been to the assumptions of Jesus' Jewish contemporaries. A "good Samaritan" would have been a contradiction in terms. There was a long history of mutual antagonism between the Jews and the Samaritans. The Samaritans were seen as engaging in an idolatrous blending of pagan culture and religious faith.

Yet this is precisely the assumption that the parable turns on its head: the despised neighbor, the Samaritan, is used to illustrate the true meaning of neighbor-love. The teaching creates a paradox in relation to a basic assumption of the audience: Samaritans are immoral and irreligious; Jews—especially religious Jews—embody God's will. Jesus' parable contradicts this assumption and, thereby, calls into question the whole logic on which it depends. He invites his hearers to move to a new frame of reference in which love of neighbor is not bound by religious and social convention.

The use of paradox lies at the heart of teaching for mystery. In this kind of teaching, we use paradoxes to

challenge the assumptions of our students' taken-for-
granted world. Two types of teaching can be described
that build on this understanding of the role of paradox.
Certainly, these are not the only two that can be pointed
to.[9] Others are described in books contained in the
Suggested Reading list. However, I have found these
two teaching approaches to be particularly useful.

The first is called *reframing*. This approach challenges
the current frame of reference that students are using to
understand their relationship with God by treating an
assumption of this frame in a paradoxical fashion. Students are encouraged to see that this paradox can only be
resolved by moving to a new frame of reference. It then
invites them to develop awareness of the new frame as a
frame, helping them see that all human knowledge of
God is finite and limited. The second type of teaching is
called *teaching contraries*. This approach introduces students to two seemingly contradictory perspectives on a
topic and then confronts them with the anomalies (things
that cannot be explained) of each perspective.

The differences between these two approaches will
become clearer as we work our way through this chapter. For the present, they can be compared in terms of
an analogy. Imagine a large, winding villa with an inner,
open-air courtyard. Different windows open on to the
courtyard, framing what can be seen in vastly different
ways. From one window, a beautiful statue can be seen.
From another, a garden comes into view. From still
another, an open archway, connecting the courtyard to
the outer world, is clearly seen. Each of these windows
affords a different perspective on what can be seen.
Reframing helps students move from one window to
another, teaching them to appreciate the view a new

perspective offers and making them aware of different perspectives. Teaching contraries helps students recognize that all the windows are limited in what they reveal and that a clear understanding of what is present in the courtyard can only be gained by viewing it from as many windows as possible.

Reframing

Reframing is based on the insight that all human knowing takes place in terms of basic frames of reference. Whether we are attempting scientific research on plants or seeking to understand God by studying the Bible, we always use basic frames of reference which influence what we see. One of the best-known illustrations of this principle is offered by the philosopher, Ludwig Wittgenstein.[10] When you look at the following picture,* what do you see?

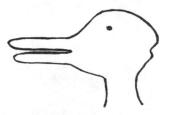

Figure 6.1

When I have asked this question of students and church groups, most people start off seeing a duck or a

---

*From Ludwig Wittgenstein, *Philosophical Investigations,* trans. G. E. M. Anscombe (Oxford: Basil Blackwell, 1968), p. 194.

platypus. Then I ask them to look for a rabbit. After a brief pause, most people can see it fairly easily. Suddenly, different parts of the picture take on different meanings. The beak becomes ears. The small indentation in the back of the duck's head becomes a mouth. What this illustrates is the importance of frames of reference in our understanding. We organize the details of what we see in terms of the larger whole or pattern that a frame provides. When we see a duck, we organize the details of the picture one way. When we see a rabbit, we organize them quite differently.

Sometimes, it is almost impossible to change the way we approach something until we shift our frame of reference. This is illustrated in another well-known exercise, the nine dot problem.[11]

Figure 6.2

In this exercise, the task is the following: Connect the nine dots by drawing four straight lines without lifting the pencil. If you have never encountered this problem, stop for a minute and try to solve it. When you are finished, turn to the next page and see how it is solved.

When people try to solve this problem for the first time, most of them view the dots as a box and try to stay within the box to draw four lines. This way of approaching the problem is based on an assumption not given in the instructions. In fact, the only way to solve the problem is to discard this assumption and adopt a new frame of reference which is not confined by the dot-box.

Scholars who have studied the process of creativity have come to the conclusion that at the heart of the creative process is a sudden leap from one frame of reference to another.[12] Items that have been viewed in one way are suddenly seen in a completely new light. It is as if a kaleidoscope has been turned and the colored pieces of glass at the end of the tube are suddenly formed into a new pattern.

Reframing focuses on helping our students begin the shift from one frame of reference to another. It challenges basic assumptions of a student's current frame of reference through the use of paradox. The key is creating a sense of contradiction within the present frame of reference that leads the person to a new frame.

One way of solving the nine dot problem is as follows:

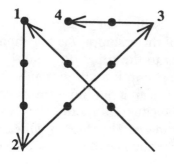

Figure 6.3

One story that illustrates this process quite nicely is about a man with a particularly bad stammer.[13] Through unexpected circumstances, this man was forced to take a job as a salesperson. As we might imagine, he was quite concerned. Like most of us, he thought of people in sales as smooth-talking individuals who can convince others to buy their products whether they are needed or not. His anxiety grew so intense he sought counseling.

The way this man's therapist approached his problem is instructive. The therapist introduced a paradox that contradicted one of the most important assumptions of the man's current frame. The therapist pointed out that his stammering was an advantage, not a liability. Almost automatically, he noted, people listen more closely to a person who has difficulty speaking. On the other hand, they are apt to turn off a smooth-talking salesperson delivering a rapid-fire barrage of words aimed at convincing them to buy things they may or may not need. The therapist went so far as to tell the man that he should maintain a high level of stammering, even if his anxiety were to diminish and he were able to speak more clearly.

The solution is illogical, weird—in short, paradoxical—in terms of the assumptions this man (and most of us) would bring to the situation. The therapist contradicted a basic assumption in the man's initial frame by labeling his handicap a potential resource. This led the man to view the situation in an entirely different way, that is, to reframe it. The duck is changed to a rabbit! The lines are extended beyond the square created by the dots!

How does this take place in teaching? The key involves creating a paradox within a student's current frame of reference that can only be resolved by shifting to a new frame of reference. This, of course, is why this process is called reframing. Paradoxes have the effect of creating a contradiction that cannot be overcome within the student's current way of viewing things. Sometimes this creates frustration and dissatisfaction. At other times, it produces a sense of relief, especially if the current frame is causing distress. In either case, a "crack" of sorts is created in the current frame, motivating the student to look for something new.

Helping persons move from one frame of reference to another, however, is only one part of reframing, as it is described here. This is because teaching for mystery is an attempt to help persons recognize the limits of their understandings of God. Shifting to a new frame does not necessarily have this effect. Sometimes people hold on to the new frame as if it were the absolute truth. A student from a fundamentalist background, for example, suddenly sees the truth of liberation theology and becomes an ardent, uncritical advocate of this perspective. Or, similarly, a college student brought up in a liberal church undergoes a conversion through her participation in an evangelical Christian group on campus and rejects all points of view other than that of her new group. Even her parents are now seen as "unsaved."

Shifting to a new frame of reference does not automatically lead to an acknowledgement of mystery in faith. It can leave people more narrow and rigid than ever. This is why reframing as a form of teaching attempts to go beyond merely helping people shift from one way of understanding God to another. It attempts to help them recognize the limits of every human understanding of God. It recognizes, however, that this will be very difficult until people have had the opportunity to view God from more than one perspective.

In virtually any area of life, it is difficult for people to acknowledge the limitations of the perspective they hold if it is the only one they have known. There is much truth in the mundane adage, it is not the fish that invented the fishtank. Trapped by the walls of the tank, the fish has no way of standing outside the tank and gaining a perspective on it.

Similarly, when people have only known one perspective in a particular area, they are "trapped" by it. If they grew up in a family of liberal Democrats and have never taken seriously a different political perspective, for example, then it is virtually impossible for them to view issues from any point of view other than the one in which they were raised. The same thing is true in matters of faith. When persons have understood God and the church from only one perspective their entire life, they are virtually trapped by this perspective.

It is at this point that reframing makes its most important contribution to teaching for mystery. It can help persons move out of their current theological frame and adopt a new one. This can afford them a point of view from which to view their old perspective. It also can afford them with an awareness of the limitations of all perspectives, including the one that they just adopted.[14] It does this by linking their frame shift with reflection on the nature of frames as such, helping them develop awareness of the limited nature of all human knowledge, especially knowledge of God. More will be said about how this is done in the fourth step described below.

For purposes of planning, it might be helpful to break down this teaching approach into four parts:

1. Identify basic assumptions of the students' current frame of reference.
2. Use parabolic communication to contradict a basic assumption of their current frame of reference.
3. Help students discover a new frame of reference that makes sense out of the paradox that has been introduced.
4. Invite students to reflect upon their new frame as a frame, helping them become aware of the limits of this perspective and all perspectives.

Identify Basic Assumptions

To identify basic assumptions of our students' current frame of reference, we must do three things. First, we must engage in *active listening*. Reframing is a highly personal approach to teaching, requiring real understanding of our students. Rather than forming superficial impressions of the people we teach on the basis of a comment here or a question there, we must listen closely to what they are saying and try to discern what it reveals about their understanding of God.

While teaching, especially during discussions, it is often a good idea to focus our attention on one individual at a time. We should listen carefully to his or her language. As we listen, we should pay special attention to the religious images, stories, and ideas that make up this student's current frame of reference. Our goal is to understand his or her way of making sense out of God. We should try to stay with his or her language, rather than translating it into our own. We might want to strike up a conversation with this student outside of class to follow up on comments or insights. In short, we should listen actively to our students in order to understand them better.

The second task we have is to *identify in concrete terms*

the assumptions that make up our students' current frame of reference. An illustration is, perhaps, the best way of clarifying what this involves. The circumstances have been altered to maintain confidentiality. John Powers took part in a church Bible study group that was using the *Kerygma* study material. He came to the group with a long history of involvement in fundamentalist churches, something that began during childhood. His parents had taught him that God threatens with eternal damnation all persons who do not conform to certain "biblical" moral standards. As John put it, "I was taught that real Christians don't drink or smoke or dance. I still have the feeling that God is always looking over my shoulder telling me that I shouldn't do this or I should do that. I feel that I'm going to get a licking if I'm not perfect. Sometimes this makes me want to give up the church altogether."

John shared this information in passing in the midst of one of the Bible study sessions. By listening actively to John, the leader began to learn that one of the assumptions of his current frame is that God is wrathful and judgmental. She tried to articulate this assumption concretely, using John's own language and images in phrases like, "When we think God's going to give us a licking . . ." and "If we think that God is looking over our shoulder . . ."

Third, we should try to *discern points of dissatisfaction* students have with their current frame of reference. We are far more likely to be successful in helping students reframe their understanding of God if we can build on a sense of need already present rather than trying to create this need ourself. Trying to force people to change usually does not work. Moreover, it can degenerate into manipulation.

Reframing is risky business. None of us has the right to tear down the faith of another person. We may cast out one demon and find that seven more have rushed in to take its place. As a general (but not absolute) rule, it is best to build on the dissatisfaction our students already feel with their current frame of reference. This can be as vague as a man's lingering sense that his understanding of the Bible is an unsatisfactory holdover from childhood or a woman's occasional twinge of guilt that her personal devotional life is less than it might be. It is important for us to identify these points of dissatisfaction. This can only be done if we take the time to get to know our students in some depth.

Use Parabolic Communication

This step represents the heart of reframing. Our task is to introduce a paradox that challenges a basic assumption of our student's current frame of reference. As I have just pointed out, it makes sense to begin with an assumption the student already has begun to question, if possible. In the case of John Powers, described above, it soon became clear that he was struggling already with the highly moralistic and judgmental understanding of God he had inherited from his past. In other cases, the dissatisfaction might not be as intense or as obvious. Our job is to build on this dissatisfaction and even intensify it to the point where a challenge to the frame as a whole begins to occur.

This can take place in many different ways. I have tried to identify four techniques that can be used to challenge the assumptions of our students. These are the reversal technique, the intensification technique, the confusion technique, and the renaming technique. By no means are these the only techniques that can be used in reframing. These four provide a picture of how this approach is done rather than a definitive list.

The Reversal Technique. This technique mirrors the kind of reversal that is found in many of Jesus' parables. There are three basic steps: (1) invite students to share their assumptions about some topic; (2) in a dramatic fashion, introduce a perspective that portrays certain aspects of their present assumptions in a radically new way; and (3) invite them to compare and contrast their initial perspective with the one to which they have just been exposed. This technique can be quite powerful if the second step addresses the assumptions that have been shared initially in a compelling and imaginative way. It can elicit a shock of surprise.

Perhaps the best way to describe how these three steps work together is through an illustration. When asked to lead a workshop for the adult leaders of a congregation's senior high youth group, a woman began by using a version of the reversal technique. She started out by having the twelve participants get in small groups and identify their assumptions about what a "great" youth group would look like. She then invited the entire group to work together to form a list on the board of the characteristics of a "great" youth group. She invited the group to cluster the characteristics under major headings. The headings were as follows: enthusiastic leadership, a strong sense of community, a clear affirmation of the authority of the Bible, and active involvement in mission. This represented the first step.

She then showed the group a video called "The

Wave." In an extremely powerful and dramatic fashion, the video showed a high school class that gradually developed the kind of group loyalty and blind obedience to a leader that characterized the Hitler youth movement preceding World War II. The process started in response to a student's question in a history class about why the German people had followed Hitler and stood by passively while six million Jews were exterminated. To answer the question the teacher began an experiment with the class. They were now to be called "The Wave" and were to recruit new members. Their life as a group was to be governed by three principles: strength through discipline, strength through community, and strength through action. The youth and teacher became caught up in the experiment, and The Wave began to terrorize the high school. The video culminated in a dramatic scene in which the teacher gets the group to see the similarities between The Wave and the Hitler youth movement. This viewing of the video represents the second step of the reversal technique.

Following the video, the workshop leader moved the group into the third step. The participants were asked to look at the list they had written on the board in light of the video. They were shocked with the similarities between their description of a great youth group and the three principles that governed The Wave. They began to question their assumptions about the role of adult leadership and community in youth groups. They searched for ways to prevent the kind of group conformity that characterized The Wave from characterizing their youth group.

The key to the reversal technique is finding something dramatic to challenge the assumptions of our students in

the second step. It is important, of course, that the
assumptions they are invited to share initially be those
that are actually addressed in this step.

The Intensification Technique. Many times people
hold assumptions about God or the Christian life that
they have taken over from others without really thinking through what they mean if taken seriously. This
technique focuses so intensely on one assumption that
the student must come to terms with it.

An illustration of this technique is found in the
teacher's response to a situation described earlier in this
chapter: John Power's struggle to overcome the wrathful, judgmental understanding of God that was a holdover from his childhood. The teacher asked John if he
would be willing to take on a devil's advocate role in the
class while it studied the first theme of the *Kerygma*
material, "God Saves His People." As the class studied
different portions of scripture each week, he was to
point out all the instances in the text in which God's
action does not seem to be gracious or saving. He
especially was to look for instances of God's wrath and
judgment. He was to argue as hard as he could that
these represent the real message of the Bible.

It seems illogical to encourage a man who thinks of
God as frightening and judgmental to look for evidence
in the Bible that confirms this assumption. The teacher's
hope, however, was that by asking John to play this
role, he would begin to take a serious look at whether or
not the Bible really describes God primarily as wrathful
and judgmental. By having John argue again and again
for this way of thinking about God, she hoped that he
might get disgusted with this one-sided perspective and

•

open himself to the more central message of grace that the Bible teaches.

Clearly, this approach is paradoxical. The teacher was asking John to advocate the very thing that he wanted to change. Through a process of intensification, it is hoped the assumption will lose its hold on the person. This is what happened in John's case. By the fourth session, he announced to the class that he was tired of advocating God's judgment and would gladly hand that role over to someone else. "I don't believe it anymore anyway," he added.

It is important to point out that John had expressed already some dissatisfaction with the assumption that the teacher made the focus of intensification. She was not asking a true believer to argue for beliefs held with complete and utter devotion. It is doubtful that the intensification technique would have worked if that had been the case. With John, it was more like asking a man to eat a steady diet of food that he does not like all that much in the first place. By the fourth or fifth meal, he is ready for a switch.

The Confusion Technique. This technique is especially useful in getting individuals or groups to examine one of their assumptions from a point of view they are likely to resist. The approach is relatively simple, although its success depends on several conditions. The teacher starts with a relatively simple and clear presentation of the point of view that will challenge one of the group's assumptions and, gradually, makes the presentation more and more complex. Eventually, the presentation reaches a level of abstraction and complexity that almost no one in the class can follow. The teacher is intentionally trying to confuse the class.

What is the purpose of creating confusion? The purpose of this technique is to get the class to forget temporarily its resistance to the point of view being presented and, out of a sense of frustration, to work hard at understanding and expressing what is at stake in it. The pay-off comes during the students' response to the confusion that has been created. The teacher turns to the class, now full of frustrated and blank faces, and says something like: "It appears that I have failed in trying to get you to understand this topic. Please form small groups and see if you can work together to state more clearly what I have been trying to say." The students are so frustrated and confused that they often are quite willing to clarify the topic. Temporarily, they forget it represents a perspective they do not like.

If the teacher wants to heighten the group's frustration, he or she circulates from group to group and offers more highly confusing statements. Something like this will do: "I forgot to mention this . . ." and then shares more incomprehensible information, moving on to the next group before the participants have a chance to ask questions. After a period of time, the teacher calls the students back together and asks them to share what they have learned.

This technique does not always work. It is helpful if we have some persistent and good thinkers in the class. For them, confusion is not acceptable. They will respond to the challenge created by our confusion and work hard to clarify what we are trying to say. It also is important for us to provide enough information about the topic in the initial portion of our presentation to give the students some idea of what we have in mind. We start clearly and only gradually move toward confusion.

I saw the confusion technique used by a theology professor who had been asked to speak to a very liberal church on the uniqueness of Christianity. His presentation was one session in a five-week series on the topic: "Jesus: One or Many Paths to God?" A different speaker was to come each week. The professor decided to focus on the uniqueness of Jesus' saving work, culminating in his death on the cross, a position that he knew would not be welcomed by the congregation. He started with a relatively brief and clear explanation of the doctrine of the atonement focusing on the importance of Jesus' death in his saving work and noting the basis of this doctrine in scripture. He gradually became more and more complex, ending with a statement like this: "Clearly, the threats of nonbeing that are an inherent part of the existential condition of humanity cannot be overcome by being itself. They represent an irresolvable ontological dilemma. This dilemma can only be overcome by something outside of the tensions that are part of the human condition. This is the purpose of Jesus' saving work and the reason that it is unique among the world religions. The more difficult question is not whether Jesus' work is uniquely saving, but did God sin in creation? Theology, to the extent that it takes ontology seriously, is driven to this question."

Perhaps people with specialized theological or philosophical training could follow this train of thought but not an average group of laypeople. The audience clearly was restless and frustrated by the end of the professor's twenty-minute presentation. He concluded with an apology for his confusing language, something he described as one of many "hazards" of his profession. He then asked them to break into groups of three or four and see if they could clarify what he had been trying to say. "I'm sure you can put it better than I," he said. The groups quickly were deep in conversation.

When the professor called them back together and asked them to share what they had come up with, three or four persons offered extremely articulate descriptions of the uniqueness of Jesus' saving work on the cross. The professor built on these statements to expand what was at stake in this perspective, staying close to the language the participants offered themselves.

Renaming Technique. Over the past decade, the power of words to name and shape reality increasingly has been recognized. Perhaps the most dramatic instance of this has been the attempt to use inclusive language in worship, in the translation of scripture, and in our everyday lives. The renaming technique is based on a recognition of the power of words to name experience. Its basic goal is quite simple: to provide people with new words to rename the realities of their lives.

In most cases, the renaming technique involves three distinct steps. In the first step, the teacher invites students to share with others their understanding of the subject being studied. The purpose of this step is to surface the key words or phrases used by students to name their understanding of the subject. The second step involves helping them become aware of the words they are using. In many ways, it is similar to the reflective aspect described in the previous chapter, only now the focus is on helping them stand back and reflect on their language. The third step focuses on the introduction of new concepts that students can use to rename their experience and to construct a new frame of reference.

I witnessed a well-known researcher and writer in the area of women's development use this technique to perfection in a conference. Instead of starting right in with the lecture she had been invited to give, she invited the audience to break into groups of two or three to discuss the following question: What is the one thing in your life you would most hate to lose? After a brief period, she asked five women to share their answers and then five men. The differences between the men and women were startling. The women's responses all had to do with relationships; the men's, with career.

The lecturer then asked the women how they felt about the difference between their answers and those of the men. Four out of five expressed mixed feelings about their answers, wondering if they should have "more important" things to do with their lives than concern themselves with their families, friends, or co-workers. Only at this point, did the leader begin her lecture. In essence, she renamed the experience of these women in terms of her research on women's development. The ongoing importance of relationships was described as a key dimension of women's development, something not acknowledged in most psychological theories. The fact that the women, who had shared prior to the lecture, felt somewhat bad about their preoccupation with relational issues was an indication that women's development was not valued in the same way as men's, leading to a crisis of self-esteem in many women. She went on to describe a whole new way of thinking about human growth and maturity.

There are a variety of ways to carry out this technique. Instead of renaming through a modified lecture, other media can be used: books, articles, or video tapes. The key is to find something that can provide a new set of concepts that renames the experience shared in the initial step. This input works best if it provides a kind of "twist" to the initial sharing. In the situation described above, for example, the women's mixed feelings about the importance of relationships was suddenly given a new "twist" in light of the lecturer's research and theory. New names were substituted for old ones.

Help Students Discover a New Frame of Reference

In each of the techniques described in the second step a paradox was introduced into the student's current frame of reference, challenging certain assumptions of this frame. The third step focuses on helping the student discover a new frame of reference that can make sense out of this paradox. It invites the student to "reframe" his or her understanding of God or some part of the Christian life.

Recall the principle stated along with the duck/rabbit picture and the nine dot exercise: Particulars are organized in terms of a larger whole. Think of a person's frame of reference as a complex set of particular assumptions woven together into a larger whole. When one of these assumptions no longer makes sense, readiness for a frame shift often begins to emerge. The motivation for changing frames is even greater if we have focused on points of dissatisfaction a person already feels toward his or her current frame. Our job in the third step is to build on this dissatisfaction and readiness to change, helping our students construct new frames. Since great variety exists in how this is done, I will illustrate this third step in terms of examples given in the previous section.

In portraying the reversal technique, I described a workshop in which the adult leaders of a youth group viewed a video called "The Wave." This video challenged them to rethink their assumptions about the kind of community and adult leadership that youth need. Constructing a new frame about youth, however, goes one step further. It involves learning to view youth in terms of a different set of assumptions.

Quite naturally, the workshop leader could have provided the participants with an introduction to adolescent development and the place of youth in contemporary American culture. The youth leaders could have learned something about the stultifying power of the peer group during adolescence and the way that youth culture often reinforces conformity to negative group values and beliefs. On the basis of their new frame, the leaders might have learned how important it is to help youth resist this "groupism," teaching them how to stand up to their peers and to appreciate the importance of individual differences.

In illustrating the intensification technique, I described how John Powers was challenged to overcome his judgmental, moralistic understanding of God by constantly arguing for this position in a Bible study group. In this case, the *Kerygma* curriculum itself provided the material for a new frame. The theme studied when the intensification technique was used was "God Saves His People." This theme allowed John to place those portions of scripture dealing with God's judgment within the more fundamental framework of God's saving action. Incidents of God's anger or judgment could be seen as attempts to discipline or redeem God's people from their self-destructive behavior rather than to destroy them. John's old frame was supplanted by a new one.

In portraying the confusion technique, I described a professor who gradually grew more and more complex in his teaching on the unique significance of Jesus' saving work on the cross. He did this to confuse his audience and to provoke them into articulating for themselves what is at stake in this theological theme, a position they were not inclined to consider. In the professor's responses to the group's sharing, he helped them construct a new frame. He stated clearly and simply the meaning of the doctrine of the atonement, its foundation in scripture, why it has been seen as central to the Christian tradition over the centuries, and the universalistic thrust of this doctrine (i.e., Christ died for *all*). In short, he carried the process of reframing through the third step.

In describing the renaming technique, I shared an example of a lecturer who was able to provide her audience with a new way of viewing the importance of relationships in women's development. In this example, she moved to the third step as part of the renaming process, providing a full-blown theory of women's development that served as an alternative to the ways human development is normally viewed. The third step is not always achieved in this way, however. Frequently, the initial process of renaming must be expanded and deepened in an additional step. In the second step, the participants have begun to acquire a new vocabulary to describe their experience, but they still need further work to understand the implications of this vocabulary and how it represents a shift away from their old frame.

In each case, the special contribution of reframing's third step is clear. After all, this approach to teaching is called *re*framing. Its purpose is to help students shift from one frame of reference to another. Gaining new flashes of insight is not enough. These insights must be developed into full-blown perspectives different from those students hold already.

Invite Students to Reflect

This fourth step is an important one and represents a key part of teaching for mystery. The central emphasis of the three steps described thus far is on helping students move from one frame of reference to another. This is important, for it provides them with more than one perspective on God and the Christian life, something that is needed when persons have viewed God in only one way. The fourth step is an attempt to use this frame shift as an occasion for reflection upon the nature of frames as such. The goal is to create a context in which students do more than see God or the Christian life in a new way. It is to help them become aware that every way of viewing God takes place within the constraints of a certain frame.

An analogy might be helpful. When taking pictures, good photographers are aware not only of the subject whose picture is being taken but also of the way the picture is being framed. Skill in framing marks the difference between an amateur and an expert photographer. At a wedding reception, for example, a professional photographer may take pictures of the same subject—the bride, for example—many times. But he or she attempts to frame this subject in many different ways, showing her in different situations, with different backgrounds, and in different light. Sometimes, the photographer may even use different lenses—a wide-angle lens or a telephoto lens—that creates dramatically different frames. In short, an expert photographer is concerned, not only with the subject of the picture, but also, with how the subject is framed.

This fourth step is an attempt to help our students become more aware of the activity of framing involved in all understanding of God. It attempts to use the occasion of their shift to a new frame as an opportunity to foster greater awareness of the activity of framing as such. How is this done?

Much depends on the kind of teaching that has taken place in the previous steps. Often, the fourth step grows quite naturally out of what has already taken place. For example, in our illustration of the renaming technique described under step two, we saw how a lecturer on women's development provided her audience with a totally new perspective on the differences between men and women's development. An important part of her lecture compared and contrasted emerging theories of women's development and more established theories that reflected men's experience. It would not have been difficult for this woman to complete her lecture by pointing out the role of guiding models in all scientific research, including her own, and the need to keep her own research in dialogue with older models of development and newer ones that were emerging.

This illustrates one technique that is often useful in the fourth step: comparing and contrasting. The emergence of a new frame is followed by a period in which it is compared and contrasted with the old frame as well as alternative new frames. Instead of advocating her own theory as a kind of ideology that should be accepted as the absolute truth, for example, the lecturer could draw comparisons and contrasts with other models to highlight the limitations of every model, including her own. The students would be invited to become aware of the process of framing that is taking place.

A second technique also useful in the fourth step involves helping the students locate their new frame in a historical context. Often this has the effect of allowing them to see that it arose in response to a particular set of circumstances and needs. The way it frames things is shaped by this historical context. Under the confusion technique described in step two, for example, a professor focused on teaching a reluctant class the special significance of Jesus' death on the cross. Having introduced this new frame, he might have indicated that this theological perspective, while found in scripture and Christian tradition, received classic expression in the writing of the medieval theologian, Anselm. It might also be noted that it is not the only way that Jesus' death has been understood in Christian theology across the ages.

The purpose in both these techniques and in others like them is to help students reflect upon the process of framing as such. Not only does this help them become aware of the limitations of the new frame they have adopted, but also, of all frames. It is an important part of the reframing technique.

Summary

As a way of concluding this discussion of reframing, a summary can be provided.

1. Identify the basic assumptions of the students' current frame of reference.
   —Listen actively to the students, paying attention to their language about God and the Christian life.
   —Identify the assumptions lying behind this language in concrete terms.
   —Discern points of student dissatisfaction with their current frames of reference.
2. Use parabolic communication to contradict a basic assumption of the students' current frame of reference.
   —Introduce a paradox which contradicts one of their assumptions.
   —Possible techniques are
      the reversal technique
      the intensification technique
      the confusion technique
      the renaming technique
3. Help students discover a new frame of reference that makes sense out of the paradox that has been introduced:
   —Help them go beyond their initial insights.
   —Build on dissatisfaction with their current frame.
4. Invite students to reflect upon their new frame as a frame, helping them become aware of the limits of this perspective and all perspectives.
   —Use techniques that flow out of the previous steps.
   —Two possible techniques are
      comparing and contrasting new and old frames
      placing the new frame in its historical context

Teaching Contraries

Reframing is an approach that is especially useful when teaching people who have had little exposure to different understandings of God and the Christian life. It provides them with the opportunity to shift to a new frame of reference, affording them a perspective on their previously held understandings of God. A context is created in which they can gain some awareness of the limitations not only of their former frame and new frame but also of all frames. This, of course, is the primary goal of teaching for mystery. In many ways, this goal is sought more directly in the second teaching approach we are going to describe: teaching contraries.

Teaching contraries receives its name from the fact that it teaches two different perspectives simultaneously (hence, "contraries") and, then, introduces anomalies that are part of each perspective. It uses paradox on a level different from reframing. Paradox is used, not so much to call into question the assumptions of a given frame but to call into question the adequacy of *every* frame. Students are invited to think paradoxically. They are encouraged to adopt a paradoxical stance in their understanding of God, holding different, even contradictory understandings of God in tension at the same time.

It is important to point out that this is not a position of relativism, so common in our society today. Relativism asserts that one position is as good as another. In religion it usually takes the form of affirming all faiths and theologies as equally valid. Paradoxical understanding, as I am using it here, is quite different. It is based on the belief that Jesus Christ is the final and unsurpassable revelation of God. It is also based on the belief that some descriptions of the God revealed by Christ are better than others. It denies, however, that any of these descriptions are absolute and complete. They remain human forms of understanding and dare not transgress the limits which surround the divine mystery.

Paradoxical understanding, as found in teaching contraries, affirms that no one perspective on God is absolute. This teaching approach intentionally places two different perspectives side-by-side, affirming the importance of both. It then exposes students to anomalies in each perspective. It invites students to hold these two perspectives in tension without reducing one to the other. The limits of human reason are acknowledged, and the mystery of God is affirmed.

The basic steps involved in teaching contraries can be outlined as follows:

1. Identify two equally valid perspectives on the topic that is being studied.
2. Teach both perspectives to the students, making sure they understand the similarities and differences.
3. Point to anomalies in each perspective.
4. Invite the students to acknowledge the strengths and weaknesses of each perspective.
5. Articulate the importance of acknowledging the mystery that surrounds God and the limits of all perspectives on God.

I will develop my description of each of these steps in relation to an example. Imagine that we have been asked to teach a series in our church entitled "The Spiritual Life: Growing in the Life of Faith." Many denominations have become interested in recent years in supporting the personal spirituality of their members. The course we have been invited to teach is one of several offerings by the congregation on this topic. We are asked specifically to help the church gain a clear understanding of what growth in the Christian life looks like in our particular denominational tradition. For the sake of being concrete, imagine that our denomination is Presbyterian. Let's see how we might approach this sort of course when using the teaching contraries approach.

Identify Two Perspectives

The first thing we must do is learn something about the subject we are to teach. Let's hope we have been asked to teach because we know something about this topic already. If this is not the case, then we should consult with knowledgeable persons and read relevant books. We should approach these resources with one primary aim in mind: to locate two different perspectives on the topic that are equally valid.

In terms of the example being developed, we would need to make a fundamental decision: Do we want these two perspectives to represent different positions in our denominational tradition or do we want to contrast our denomination's understanding of the spiritual life with that of a different denomination? For the sake of developing this example, let's say that we have decided to present different perspectives from within our own denominational tradition. After reading several books on this topic and talking with several people, we identify two contrasting perspectives that have some relevance to our class's experience.

The Presbyterian church, we discover, experienced a major division at one point in American history between "New School" Presbyterians and "Old School" Presbyterians. The New School position, especially that wing influenced by revivalism, placed great emphasis on personal religious experience, particularly conversion experience. The Old School position viewed the Christian life as a gradual, unfolding process within the covenant community.[15]

If we stop to think about it, most subjects in the church could be approached from at least two different perspectives. It is often a matter of knowing our subject well enough to identify these perspectives. In teaching contraries, this is the first and, perhaps, most important step we take.

Teach Both Perspectives

Having identified two perspectives, our next task is to decide how we are going to present them. We might well draw on different methods described in earlier chapters of this book, using a lecture format or leading a discussion that deals with assigned reading. The important point is to *present each position as equally valid*.

As a teacher, we should probably try to remain neutral. At a later point, we may decide to reveal our own preference, but this is probably not wise at the outset. Our task is to present each position in as compelling a manner as possible. If we make our own position known, some students almost always will prefer this position to please us or, on the contrary, will challenge this position as an indirect way of challenging our authority. Remaining neutral makes it easier for our students to enter into each perspective.

Our task is to help our students get inside both perspectives. If students begin to criticize a perspective before they have really tried to understand it, we must gently but firmly encourage them to put aside their criticisms for a while and try to enter into this perspective sympathetically. We might encourage them to listen closely to others in the group who are doing a better job at this.

We must make sure that the class begins to see the contribution each perspective has to make. In the example we are developing, let's imagine we have decided to spend two weeks covering this step and have chosen two formats to do so. In the first session, we use a lecture format to place the New School/Old School controversy in its original historical context. We use a discussion period at the end of the lecture primarily for questions of clarification. In the second week, we use a focused discussion format to go over a small amount of assigned reading. We attempt to guide the discussion from a consideration of the New School and Old School controversy in its original context to the ways this controversy continues to exist today. We work hard to make sure the class is able to articulate each side's understanding of the spiritual life. We discourage critical evaluation and debate at this point.

Point to Anomalies

Once our class has understood each perspective, our task is to introduce anomalies. An anomaly is something that cannot be explained adequately from within a particular frame of reference.[16] It focuses on what scientists sometimes call "discrepant data." These are findings that cannot be explained by the theories guiding a research project. Certain parts of the data simply do not conform with the researcher's expectations. Every theory, no matter how well established, has certain unexplainable anomalies.

Our task in this step is to make apparent the anomalies

of the two perspectives the group is examining. We are not yet inviting our students to evaluate the strengths and weaknesses of each position, but we are confronting them with the limitations of each perspective. Remember, our long-term goal is not only to help them confront the limits of these two perspectives but also of every perspective.

To continue our example, the New School perspective, especially in its revivalistic forms, repeatedly has been plagued by an individualistic view of salvation and a preoccupation with the moment of conversion. The issues it seems unable to deal with adequately are the contribution of the church and the way that it shapes the life of faith both before and after conversion. In contrast, the Old School position has had great difficulty resisting authoritarianism and social conformity in its desire for church unity. The issues it seems unable to deal with adequately are the legitimate place of individual dissent and pluralism in the church community. It has tended to confuse unity with uniformity.

To teach the third step, we decide to use a mixed discussion format to get at these issues. We begin by stating these anomalies in a brief lecture, documenting their appearance historically. We then open the discussion portion of the session by saying: "Let's see if we can figure out why each position has had so much difficulty with these issues. Let's start with the New School position and then move to the Old School position." Gradually, we invite the class to share examples of these weaknesses in the contemporary offspring of these two positions. During the discussion, we begin to label the New School position, the "crisis pattern" of the spiritual life, and the Old School position, the "growth in community" pattern.

Invite Students to Assess Each Perspective

Having invited our students to enter into each perspective and having introduced certain anomalies, our task now is to help them assess these perspectives. Ideally, our students will have a sense of the strengths and weaknesses of both positions. The purpose of teaching two positions at the same time is to prevent our students from accepting only one perspective on the subject they are studying. Even if they favor one position over the other, they should be able to acknowledge its limitations. We hope they can see that the perspective they do not prefer can handle some things better than the one they favor.

Another way of putting this is to say that our goal is to foster paradoxical thinking. Remember, a paradox holds in tension two arguments, both of which are reasonable, that seem to contradict one another. On a broad scale, this is what we are trying to invite our students to do. We want them to see the strengths and weaknesses of both positions, helping them affirm what each has to offer while confronting them with their limitations as well.

To continue our example, we decide to carry out the fourth and fifth steps during the fourth session of the class. Many times, the third, fourth, and fifth steps flow together quite naturally and can be handled at the same time. In this case, we decide we want to spend a substantial amount of time helping our class come to terms with the strengths and weaknesses of both positions. This is especially important because something similar to each position is present in the congregation. By helping the students achieve a paradoxical understanding of their denomination's understanding of the spiritual life, we would strengthen mutual understanding in the congregation.

We begin with a brief review of the important ideas covered to that point in the series, reminding the students of our description of the New School position as a "crisis pattern" and the Old School position as a "growth in community" pattern. We then ask the class to list the strengths and weaknesses of each position, while writing them down on newsprint. Dividing the class into small groups, we then ask them to come up with a brief paragraph that summarizes their assessment of each position. These summaries are to include both positive and negative characteristics. We gather the groups together and ask several of them to share what they have written. Following this, we shift to the final step.

Acknowledge the Mystery That Surrounds God

At some point in teaching contraries we must make clear to our class that there is a theological basis for the way we have approached the subject. The goal is to connect their critical appreciation of two different perspectives on the Christian life with a theological affirmation of the mystery that is a part of faith.

This is important for one basic reason: to help them generalize what they have learned in the class to other areas. The best kind of teaching almost always does more than help students learn skills or ideas that can only be used in the particular setting in which they were learned. Rather, what is learned can be generalized to other, somewhat different settings and topics.

Teaching people to generalize is especially important in the church, where the goal is to help people move outside the classroom and apply what they have learned to the rest of their lives. In teaching contraries, our goal is to teach them to appreciate the mystery that surrounds God and the limits that are a part of every perspective on God. Having learned this at one point in relation to one subject, our students, we hope, will be able to generalize this theological concept to other issues.

It is important, thus, at some point in teaching contraries that we make a direct link between the way we have taught the subject and the theological concept that undergirds it. In the example being developed, we decide to do this in the following way. Having invited several of the small groups to share their brief summary statements about the crisis and growth patterns, we then ask the class, "Why do you think it is important for us to affirm the validity of both perspectives in our church?"

After receiving several answers, we then read part of Romans 12: "For by the grace given to me I say to everyone among you not to think of yourself more highly than you ought to think, but to think with sober judgment, each according to the measure of faith that God has assigned. For as in one body we have many members, and not all the members have the same function, so we, who are many, are one body in Christ, and individually we are members one of another" (Rom. 12:3–5). We then ask, "Why do you think Paul invites the Christians in Rome and us today 'not to think of yourself more highly than you ought to think'?"

After several responses, we ask, "In light of what we learned about the Christian life in this class, what does

Paul tell us about affirming different perspectives in the church?" We conclude by linking the students' responses to the theological idea of God as mystery, an idea that invites us to acknowledge the limits that are part of every perspective on God. Not thinking too highly of yourself and relying on the diversity in the Christian community, we point out, is a way of acknowledging the mystery that is part of faith.

By linking the idea of mystery directly to Paul's description of the church as a body with many parts, we encourage the class to look beyond the topic studied to the ongoing life of the church. The class's experience of contrary positions is now grounded in more general theological concepts that can be used to understand many different situations and topics in the future.

Summary

The various steps involved in teaching contraries can be summarized as follows:

1. Identify two equally valid perspectives on the topic that is being studied.
    —Through conversation with others or reading, identify several different perspectives on the subject being taught.
    —Decide on two perspectives that approach the subject differently and are in tension with one another.
2. Teach both perspectives to the students, making sure they understand their similarities and differences.
    —Decide on the teaching methods (lecture, discussion, etc.) that can be used to teach these two perspectives.
    —Remain neutral toward both perspectives when they are first presented.

—Work hard to make sure students understand and appreciate both perspectives.

3. Point to anomalies in each perspective.

—Intentionally identify or help the students identify important issues that each position has a great deal of difficulty explaining.

—Work hard to make sure the students understand and appreciate the anomalies in both positions, not just the one they like least.

4. Invite students to acknowledge the strengths and weaknesses of each perspective.

—Focus on a critical assessment of each position.

—Invite students to state for themselves the positive and negative aspects of each position.

—Once more, encourage students to be fair to each position.

—Encourage them to think paradoxically.

5. Articulate the importance of acknowledging the mystery that surrounds God and the limits of all perspectives on God.

—Link the class's experience of paradox to a theological affirmation of the mystery surrounding God and the limits of all human understanding of God.

—Invite the class to generalize this theological insight to other situations or topics they might face as Christians.

7

Teaching Yourself
or Others
with This Book

This chapter has two purposes. First, it is designed for people who would like to use this book to improve their teaching in an intentional fashion. Second, it is written for church leaders who are responsible for educating teachers on an ongoing fashion. Accordingly, the first part of the chapter identifies several basic principles that can help people use this book to improve their teaching over time. The second part focuses on some of the basic ideas of the book and how they might be presented in workshops.

Improving Our Teaching: A Long-term Project

This book began by pointing out that most of us can become good teachers only by working at it over time. We have to try new methods; we have to fail; and then we have to try again. If something does not work at first, we should not be afraid to try it again. Few things in life can be learned quickly and easily. We need to take the long view. Improvement will come if we work at it and are willing to take some risks.

Taking the long view is important for another reason. It saves us from trying out too many new ideas at one time with our class. Ideally, churches should have periodic lab schools in which teachers can try out new teaching approaches with other teachers. Most of the time we will not have this luxury, however. We will have to try out new ideas with our own class. If we do this too often, however, it will be frustrating for our students. Taking the long view allows us to slip in a new technique here and a new method there. Our task is to enhance our teaching repertoire over time.

As we work on improving our teaching over time, we need to keep in mind the following admonitions.

Build on Our Strengths

This principle is extremely important. While it is not a good idea to try out several new teaching methods in close succession with our class, this does not mean we cannot work at improving our teaching every time we teach. We can work at building on our strengths. Almost all of us are better at some aspects of teaching than at others. Some people are diligent in their advance preparation, reading new material for each class. Others think quickly on their feet and are good at building on student responses to their questions.

We should try to be honest with ourselves. What are our strengths? What do we do well? What do we like to do most in our teaching? We should try to build on these strengths every time we teach. If we enjoy leading a discussion and do it reasonably well, then we might focus on improving this part of our teaching. We might reread the chapter on leading a good discussion and pick out one area to work on: writing different kinds of questions, for example. We might focus on this area for several weeks in a row, paying attention to how the class responds to different types of questions. Which type of question takes longer to respond to? Which type gets the best discussion going? We might experiment with placing the questions in a different order, starting with provocative, evaluative questions one week and factual ones the next. Once we have developed some competence in question-asking, we might turn to a different aspect of leading a discussion. Perhaps we have never tried an open-ended discussion. We might reread the section of this book dealing with this type of discussion and try out the ideas, using the approach several times.

Building on our strengths is perhaps the safest way to improve our teaching. It allows us to develop expertise in certain areas gradually. In the long run, this gives us the confidence to work at those aspects of teaching that we do not do well.

Develop "Bread and Butter" Teaching Methods

This is a direct outgrowth of the principle described immediately above. We should think in terms of developing "bread and butter" teaching methods. These are methods that make use of our strengths and ones we have some experience using. Rather than trying to improve our teaching in all areas described in this book, we focus on one or two methods and work on learning how to use them with confidence and competence. Once we have developed "bread and butter" approaches, we can gradually begin to expand our repertoire.

Plan Ahead

Planning is always important in teaching and even more important when we are trying to improve our teaching in a systematic way. It is probably a good idea to plan which teaching methods we will use each quarter. We might look over the topics to be covered during the coming quarter. Which teaching methods seem to go best with which subjects?

Planning in this way provides us with an overview of the ways we are teaching faith over a period of time. Are we addressing more than one side of the faith cube? Are we always focusing on the relational side of faith? Do we ever provide our students with new information that can deepen their beliefs? Addressing more than one side of the faith cube is hard to do if we are working at developing one or two "bread and butter" teaching approaches. Nonetheless, it is important to become aware of the primary ways we are supporting and challenging faith in our teaching, so we can broaden the focus of our teaching over time.

Design Detailed Lesson Plans

Ideally, we should design a detailed lesson plan for every session we teach. It is especially important to write out a lesson plan when we are trying a new teaching method. This helps us think through the learning activities we will use and project how much time each will take. After the session, we can use the plan to evaluate how things went. Did we achieve our basic goals? Did some activities take longer than we had anticipated?

It is easy to create a planning sheet. Some teachers find it helpful to begin by listing several basic categories at the top of the sheet. A category like "Subject," for example, might refer to the general topic the lesson deals with. Similarly, "Teaching Method" might refer to the teaching method to be used: lecture, focused discussion, reframing, and so on. "Session Goals" might refer to the specific information or insights the teachers hope their students will learn. Under general categories like these, many teachers find it helpful to write down the learning activities they will use, the time they will need for each activity, and the kinds of resources that should be available for each activity. This serves as a concrete plan of action to guide their teaching.

Search for New Ideas

Throughout this book, I have repeatedly pointed out that the teaching methods described here are only a fraction of those available. An important part of improving our teaching is to continue to read books about teaching that can expose us to new methods and ideas. (An annotated Suggested Reading list is included at the back of this book.)

Just as important as reading about teaching is experiencing good teaching on a firsthand basis. Often this is not easy for teachers, because they cannot attend other classes while they are teaching themselves. If at all possible, however, it is a good idea to find ways of participating in other classes at least occasionally. Sometimes churches offer classes on Sunday evening or during the week. If your church does not, scout around for one that does. Consider borrowing a video that is designed for teaching. Attending class at a nearby community college or university might be an option.

Not only is this sort of participation important for our continued growth as a person and as a teacher, but also we can pick up new ideas by watching others teach. There is no better way to learn how to lecture well than by watching a good lecturer. The same is true of other teaching methods. Sometimes it is best not to listen to what is being taught but to focus on how it is being taught. What is the teacher doing right? What could be improved? Developing this evaluative capacity toward others allows us to become a better evaluator of our own teaching.

Consult with Others

We can learn not only a great deal by watching others teach but also by consulting with other teachers when we run into problems. Some churches designate certain experienced teachers as "trouble shooters." They can be called on to observe a class when a teacher is having trouble with a person who talks too much or is finding the curriculum difficult to use. Ideally, we can call on a specialist in Christian education, either a Christian educator or the minister. Unfortunately, this is not possible in every church. If it is not possible to ask one of the leaders of the church for help, we might try to find an experienced public school teacher who can be consulted when problems are encountered. It is amazing how helpful it can be to talk about difficulties with an experienced teacher.

Teaching Others to Teach

In the remainder of this chapter, a series of sessions are described that can be used by leaders of the church to help teachers learn and practice many of the ideas contained in this book. There is no such thing as a "canned" lesson plan, one that can be pulled out and used without modification for any group. What follows are plans that can be adapted to different groups of teachers. Those of us who are involved in providing teacher training for our congregations should go beyond what is offered here. Each lesson plan is followed with some "idea starters" that can help us think of our own ways of using this material.

The basic premise lying behind all these plans is that the best way to introduce a teaching method is to model it in our teaching. In large part, this means the sessions are based on what is frequently called an action/reflection teaching method. A particular teaching approach is experienced by the workshop participants on a firsthand basis, and then they reflect on what they have experienced.

Four Dimensions of Faith: A Session
Modeling the Lecture Method

This session has two goals: (1) to introduce the students to the four dimensions of faith identified in this book, using the lecture approach, and (2) to help students identify the different parts of the lecture they have just heard.

Follow the steps for preparing a lecture described in the third chapter. Begin by reading and marking up the first three chapters of the book. On the basis of the reading, create an idea outline. At a later point, a copy of this will be handed out to the group, so write in a fairly legible fashion. On the basis of this idea outline, create the presentation outline. Be sure to structure the lecture along the lines of a clear organizing principle. Do not indicate to the students what this principle is, for they will be asked to identify it later. Also, be sure to include the different parts of the lecture mentioned in the chapter: an introduction, the body, summary/transitional statements, and a conclusion. Since examples are so important, make sure to include some good ones.

I would have about as much detail in the presentation outline as is contained in the following introduction of a sample lecture on this topic.

I. Introduction: The Many Sides of Faith
   A. What is the purpose of our teaching in the church? This is the basic question we are exploring this morning.
   B. When a high school soccer coach holds a team practice he or she tries to teach basic soccer skills. When someone teaches a quilting class at the YMCA, she or he tries to teach students how to quilt. What is the purpose of our teaching in the church?
   C. In the book we are studying today, the author gives the following answer to this question: "The basic purpose of teaching is to create a context in which faith can be awakened, supported, and challenged."
   D. The key word here is *faith*.
   E. What does the word *faith* mean to you? Give me some quick responses. (Write on newsprint or blackboard.)
   F. This is how the author defines faith: "Faith is a relationship of trust in God whose loving-kindness and faithfulness have been shown in Jesus Christ." (Write next to comments already on the board.) How does this definition compare with the ideas we put on the board?
   G. As the author unpacks this definition, he borrows an

idea from the theologian H. Richard Niebuhr.
Faith, Niebuhr says, is like a many-sided cube.
(Draw a cube on newsprint or point to a picture that
you already have drawn.)
1. Like a cube, faith has many sides.
2. Like a cube, we can only see several of the sides
   at any one time. Others remain out of view.
3. The book we are studying identifies four important sides of the faith cube: belief, relationship,
   commitment, and mystery. (Write these in the
   cube you have drawn.) There are other sides, but
   these four are a good place to start.
H. Different teaching approaches are better at addressing different sides of the faith cube.
   1. Today, we want to examine the four sides of the
      faith cube: faith as belief, as relationship, as
      commitment, and as mystery.
   2. At a later point, we will explore different teaching
      approaches that can address each side.
I. What is the purpose of teaching in the church? To
   awaken, support, and challenge faith. Let me briefly
   describe four dimensions of faith that can be the
   focus of our teaching.

Normally, I do not write out in sentence form every
point of my outline. I did so in this instance to make it
easier to follow my line of thinking more easily in this
sample introduction to a lecture. Our goal is to come up
with an outline of sufficient detail that the participants
can use it to identify different parts of the lecture. This
leads us to the second part of the session.

Once we have completed the lecture, we should have a
brief break. Afterwards, give the group the handouts of
the idea outline and the presentation outline. Briefly

describe how the idea outline was generated and, perhaps, even show the marked up book read in preparation. Then ask them to look at the presentation outline. Point out the differences between the idea outline and the presentation outline. Stress the importance of doing more than merely summarizing the ideas of the material read.

Write on the board the following important concepts: organizing principle, introduction, body, summary/ transitional statements, conclusion, and examples. After a brief description of each concept, ask the group to divide into groups of twos or threes and identify each of these in the presentation outline. If they have not read the chapter already, describe what each concept is pointing to before they work in groups. After a designated period of time, call the small groups together and ask them to identify each part of the lecture. Conclude with a brief discussion of the aspects of lecturing that cause these teachers the most fear.

Idea Starters

1. In working with a group that has already read the first three chapters of the book, you might consider handing out a lecture presentation outline instead of delivering a lecture. Review the different parts of the lecture and then ask the students to evaluate the lecture outline. Encourage them to point out what is missing or could be improved.
2. Show the group a video tape of an excellent lecturer. Periodically, stop the tape and ask participants to analyze the different parts of the lecture.
3. Spend additional time helping the group learn how to come up with examples. Assign them an extremely

abstract topic and have them work in groups of two or
three to come up with examples that could explain and
illustrate the topic. Invite them to examine a lecture
outline or a photocopied sermon and identify the examples. Ask them to evaluate them critically. Do they
communicate or distract from the main point?

Leading a Discussion: A Session on Learning How to Ask Good Questions

Learning how to ask good questions is an extremely
important skill for teachers to develop. In this session, a
focused discussion approach is used to talk about various facets of leading a discussion. This is followed by a
period of reflection on the outline of this discussion in
which the group tries to identify the four basic types of
questions as they appear in the outline.

We must first, of course, create a question outline.
Let us assume that the group has read the fourth chapter
of this book on leading a discussion. The following is a
brief portion of the sort of question outline we would
need to lead a focused discussion.

   I. Do you like to use the discussion method in teaching?
     A. When it goes well, what happens?
     B. When it goes badly, what happens?
     C. What scares you the most about using this method in
        your teaching?
  II. The book that we read describes three different types of
     discussion. What are they? (focused, open-ended, and
     mixed)
     A. What is the difference between a focused and an
        open-ended discussion?

   B. Which of you feel more comfortable with a focused discussion? Why?

   C. Which of you feel more comfortable with an open-ended discussion? Why?

   D. The author claims that most of our discussions in the church are mixed discussions? Why do you think he makes this claim?

I would include as much detail as possible in the outline. Consider including answers to some questions in parentheses and writing in some possible prompting and probing questions under questions that are likely to be difficult to answer.

Once the discussion is completed, we should give the group a break. After they have reassembled, give them a copy of the question outline. Write on the board and briefly go over the four different types of questions identified in the book: factual, analytical, productive, and evaluative. Working individually, each person is to label the different questions in the outline as one of these four types. After this, they should compare their answers in small groups. Call the total group together and invite them to share what they have come up with. Ask them to reflect on the group's response to the different questions when they originally were asked. Were they hard to answer? Did they take some active thinking on the students' part? Did the questions seem to build on one another? Were there too many of one type of question and not enough of another?

Conclude with brief reflections on the focused-discussion format. How closely did the discussion follow the question outline? Were they surprised that the group followed the outline as closely as it did? Did individuals feel that the discussion moved away from issues they would have liked to explore in greater depth in order to get through the material?

Idea Starters

1. Provide the group with a sheet of questions and have them identify the four types of questions. Or ask them to look over the question section of part of their curriculum and do the same thing.
2. After discussing the four types of questions, assign a passage of scripture and ask each person to write five minutes worth of questions, being sure to include at least one example of each type. Call the group together and ask one of the participants to lead it in a discussion of the passage, using his or her questions. Cut it off after five minutes and discuss what happened. Repeat with other people.
3. In small groups, come up with possible ways of responding to awkward situations that arise when questions are asked. How might you handle a prolonged silence? What might you say to the group? How might you get the group back on track when it gets off on a tangent? What might you say and do if one person keeps dominating the discussion? What might you do if the discussion gets too heated? How do you cool it off? Come back together in the total group and share some of the ideas you have come up with.
4. Discuss the use of different techniques that are helpful in leading a discussion: redirecting, affirming responses, probing, prompting, and giving qualifying instructions. Assign the group a Bible passage and ask each person (or pair) to come up with five minutes worth of questions. Call the group together and ask one of the participants to lead it in a discussion of the passage, attempting to use some of the techniques discussed initially. Call

time after five minutes, and invite the group to reflect on what techniques were used. It is often good to have pairs write questions together and lead the group, making it easier for one person to follow up a question with a specific discussion technique.

Life Stories and Faith Commitments: A Session Using the Open-ended Discussion Approach

In this session we have two goals: (1) helping our students gain a better understanding of the relationship between personal identity narratives and faith commitments; and (2) modeling the use of an open-ended discussion approach to teaching.

Often, people think of an open-ended discussion as easier to plan and lead than a focused discussion, for the latter requires a detailed outline. It is important to emphasize that this is not the case. If anything, leading an open-ended discussion requires more preparation. The leader must know the subject so well that he or she can move with the group in a variety of different directions. The leader also must be prepared to spark good discussion if the group members do not generate it themselves.

To emphasize the importance of preparation for an open-ended discussion, it is important to be able to share with the group the various steps we went through in preparing for this session. Follow the five steps outlined in the section focusing on an open-ended discussion. Reread chapter 5 of this book, marking it or taking notes on the chapter. Note the important ideas and questions that emerge while reflecting on these ideas. Then we should focus on the relationship of this material to our own life. Consider questions like these:

- Has your interpretation of your own life story shifted over the course of your life? What brought about these shifts?
- What does the author mean by "interpretive keys"? Can you identify the interpretive keys you used at an earlier point in your life?
- The author claims that faith commitments are not a matter of individual will as much as an outgrowth of the underlying story that people use to interpret their lives? Does this ring true to your own experience? At what point does human choice enter in?

Once we have thought about a range of issues like these in relation to our own life, we should reflect on them in terms of one or two people who are likely to be in the session. Are these people able to point to dramatic shifts in their life stories? If not, what kinds of shifts might they point to? How will these people make sense of the concept "interpretive keys"? If they are avid readers, could we ask them to identify this concept in relation to a novel? If the concept is likely to be difficult, how could we illustrate it for them? I would consider jotting down the reflections that occur. We want to form a "paper trail" that can be shared with the group after the discussion in order to show the kind of preparation involved in leading an open-ended discussion.

For similar reasons, write out in a legible manner, an idea sheet listing ideas that would be good to discuss during the session. Remember, this is not an idea outline but a sheet of ideas that might be of interest to the group. We should write on this sheet how we will start the discussion. Consider writing this out word-for-word in order to indicate to the group the importance of planning out the initial stage of this sort of discussion.

The next step is to lead the discussion. Work hard at making it genuinely open-ended. Try not to control it. Function as a facilitator, following the lead of the group, but interject ideas when appropriate. After the discussion, give the group a break, and then invite them to move into a brief time of personal reflection on the discussion. Tell them they have just experienced an open-ended discussion and briefly summarize the description given in this book. Ask them to respond silently to three questions: (1) When were you most engaged in the discussion? When least engaged? (2) If you were to describe the discussion in an image, what would it be? Come up with images like the following: a roller coaster, a long slide, or spinning in circles. (3) What do you think it is like to be the leader of this sort of discussion?

Once individuals have had time to think about these questions, invite the group to gather together and share their thoughts. In discussing the third question, share with them how you felt as leader of this particular discussion. Then share with them the various steps that were moved through in preparing for this session. Show them the outlines created while preparing. We might conclude by telling them that the author of this book believes that an open-ended discussion is dependent on the group as much as the leader. How did they do as a group? What might they do better in the future?

Idea Starters

1. Briefly discuss the different types of discussion identified in chapter 4. Divide them into groups of three or

four and assign a different type of discussion to each group. They are to plan for this type of discussion in relation to an assigned topic. Consider asking them to focus on a well-known biblical passage. Have them come together and share their outlines or idea sheets.

2. Try an exercise that teaches the leader of an open-ended discussion to depend on the group, using skills of redirection, probing, prompting, and silence. Tell the group they have five minutes to think about an assigned topic or passage. Then ask for a volunteer to lead the group in a discussion of this topic. Encourage him or her to use the group's ideas and to focus on involving others in the discussion. Reflect briefly on this discussion and then repeat, using a different topic.

Committed Teaching: A Session on Teaching for Commitment

Our basic goal is to have the group experience each of the five aspects of teaching commitment in relation to their own commitment to teaching. As we can recall, these aspects are remembering, reflecting, encountering, sharing, and deciding.

Begin by asking students to work individually on the following: Recall two or three teachers who were really important in your life. Write down a brief paragraph about each one. What made this person special? How did he or she affect you? Then invite the participants to move into small groups to share what they have come up with. Ask them to focus on only one of the teachers. After the sharing is under way, interrupt the groups and ask them to reflect on the following question once everyone has had a chance to share: In light of your group's experience, what makes a teacher a good teacher? After the groups have had a chance to discuss this, invite them back together for sharing. Write on the blackboard the general characteristics of a good teacher as they are identified by the group. Invite the group to write a brief summary paragraph describing a good teacher. Start with: "A really good teacher . . ."

Follow this with a brief break. When the participants return, provide them with a handout of several Bible passages. Each passage should show Jesus carrying out some aspect of his teaching ministry. Read each passage to the group, and ask participants which passage represents the greatest challenge to their teaching. Signs representing each passage should be posted at different points around the room. Ask them to go to the sign representing the passage they chose. They are to find another person who also has chosen this passage and discuss why they chose it.

Call the pairs together, and ask them to share briefly the most important thing this passage is saying to them. Write these on the blackboard, grouping them under the passage chosen by the different pairs. After every pair has had a chance to share, ask the group to look at what is written on the board and reflect on the challenge that Jesus' teaching ministry poses to the church today. Then invite them to look at the definition of a good teacher they created at the beginning of the session to see if they would like to add to this definition in light of their reflections.

Conclude by having them work individually on identifying one area in their teaching they would like to work on in the near future. Encourage them to be concrete and specific. Gather the entire group together, and invite them to enter into a brief closing period of worship. Read once more the Bible passages used earlier in the session, and invite individuals to share briefly what they are going to work on in the coming weeks. Conclude with prayer.

Idea Starters

1. Follow this session with a brief period in which you go over the different aspects of teaching commitment and indicate at what points they were dealt with in the session. Provide a brief session outline listing the different activities, labeling which aspect(s) was covered at which point.
2. Assign the group a topic that is to be taught using the teaching commitment approach. Divide them into small groups and ask them to design a lesson plan that uses all five of the aspects at least once in the session. After they have completed the task, call the groups back together and allow them to compare the lesson plans they have created.
3. Offer a "sampler" of different techniques that can be used with different aspects. For example, in quick succession have the group discuss something in small groups, use the concentric circle technique, and then have a brief panel discussion. Point to books that describe these techniques and others like them that are helpful in sharing. Ask the group to brainstorm other techniques they have seen used.

Commitment in the Bible: A Session on the Five Aspects of Teaching Commitment

This session is designed to help students understand the five aspects of teaching commitment: remembering, reflecting, encountering, sharing, and deciding. Begin by reviewing each of these aspects as they are found in chapter 5. Then divide the students into relatively small work groups. Each group is to find these five aspects in the life and ministry of a biblical character. Good candidates are Moses, Ruth, Paul, Jacob, Peter, Deborah, and David. Prepare a sheet on each biblical figure, listing the important Bible passages each small group should review. Ask each group to discuss the following questions:

- Can you identify each aspect of commitment in the life of this biblical figure? Try to identify specific passages that indicate remembering, reflecting, encountering, sharing, or deciding is taking place.
- What does this person have to teach us about the importance of these aspects? Are all aspects equally important in this person's life or are some more important than others? Which aspects seem to be most difficult for this person?
- The author claims that commitments shift as changes take place in the life story of a person. Do you think this is true in the person you are studying? Is it true in your own life?

After the groups have had a chance to work together, invite them to come back together and share in the larger group. This can take place in several ways, depending on the size of the group. I personally prefer many small groups in order to get everyone involved, even though this makes it more difficult to have each group share in the total group. If there are many small groups, consider having each group share only one or two insights that emerged when studying the person. If there are only a few small groups (fewer than six), consider allowing each to describe the passages they have found that indicate different aspects of commitment. Building on this sharing, the total group should discuss two basic questions: Are our commitments grounded in our life stories? Do our commitments change as we reinterpret our stories?

Idea Starters

1. Follow this Bible study by getting the small groups back together and having them plan a class that focuses on several of the aspects of teaching commitment. Ask them to identify the problems they are likely to run into.
2. Invite individual teachers to look over the material they are to teach during the coming quarter to see if they can identify a period in which they might teach for commitment. Ask them to write down the five aspects at the top of index cards and to come up with learning activities appropriate for each aspect. Then have them put the cards in the order that will be followed in their actual teaching.
3. Invite an experienced teacher who has studied chapter 5 closely to describe his or her experience of teaching for commitment. Encourage this person to share with the group why teaching for commitment is important to the life of the church as well as offer practical advice on how to get a class to participate in this approach.

Encouraging Openness to Students: A Session Using the Reversal Technique

Modeling the various techniques described in the chapter on teaching for mystery is undoubtedly the best way of enticing teachers to try them in their own teaching. This session uses the reversal technique to help teachers examine their own assumptions about the role of the student in teaching.

Begin by inviting the participants to identify the most important things teachers do to prepare for teaching. They should do this initially by themselves or with one other person. Then invite them to share their insights in the total group, write them down on newsprint or on a blackboard. Then ask the participants to group their insights into major categories. Most of the time, these insights focus on how the teacher prepares in order to do certain things to or for the students.

The next step invites them to think of their preparation in a totally new way. It is based on an activity that Maria Harris describes in both her video, "Teaching and Religious Imagination" and her book by the same title (found in the Suggested Reading). Harris invites her students to become aware of the artistry in teaching by working with a lump of clay. At one point, she even blindfolds the members of the group and invites them to "find the form" in the clay rather than imposing their own order on it. The important point for the purposes of this session is the way that Harris invites teachers to put aside their preconceived notions and work with the form that gradually emerges, following its lead, allowing it to show itself. A key part of teacher preparation is putting aside our preconceived notions of what the teacher will do to or for students and allowing the "form" of the session to emerge out of their prayerful and sympathetic appreciation of their students.

There are several ways we can carry out this step. The first is simply to do what Harris does. Give the students some clay and move them through the steps as described in her book. Alternatively, we might show the group the segment of the video in which she has the class work with the clay. Harris is a dramatic and compelling speaker, so this presentation can have the kind of power that is necessary when using the reversal technique.

The third step involves looking back at the assumptions about teacher preparation the group put on the board initially. Invite them to explore the important difference between "finding the form" in the clay and imposing order from without. How might this change their understanding of teacher preparation?

Conclude by asking them to compare and contrast Harris' understanding of students and the one they initially held. What is the truth found in each way of viewing students? Why is it important for them as teachers to expose themselves to different understandings of how people learn and grow?

Idea Starters

1. Invite individuals and then the group as a whole to share their assumptions about the role of the teacher in the classroom. Provide them with a handout of excerpts from Parker Palmer's *To Know as We Are Known* (see the Suggested Reading list) that are likely to challenge their assumptions.

2. Use excerpts from literature to reverse the expectations of the group. Wonderful ideas can be found in *Themes of Adulthood through Literature* (see Suggested Reading). In that book, for example, an excerpt from John Osborne's *The Paper Chase* is used to describe a student's devastating first day at Harvard Law School. It moves back and forth between the student's perspective to that of the professor. It could provide a wonderful reversal.

3. Use portions of videos to dramatically reverse teacher expectations. *Educating Rita* and *Dead Poets Society*, for example, provide numerous possibilities.

Final Reflections

Once more, it is important to point out that these lesson plans should be adapted to the particular group of teachers that are participating in the teacher training event. Whether we adapt these plans or come up with our own, one of the key ways of teaching others is by modeling the teaching that we would like them to learn. That is the basic premise of the plans outlined above, and it is a good idea to keep it in mind in workshop design.

Appendix: Two Patterns
for Teaching
Commitment

A Six Week Church School Class Series
on Personal Spirituality

(Each session lasts approximately fifty minutes.)

Week One

Encountering. Passages of Jesus at prayer are studied inductively. The three movements of spirituality found in Henri Nouwen's *Reaching Out* are described: from loneliness to solitude, from hostility to hospitality, and from illusion to prayer.[1]

Week Two

Remembering. On paper, each person is asked to recollect their experiences of prayer as a child and youth.

Sharing. The class is then divided into sharing groups to tell others what they have remembered.

Reflecting. The entire group is reassembled, and Nouwen's three movements are placed on newsprint. The group is asked: Which of these movements of spirituality did your past prepare you most to undertake? Which least?

Week Three

Encountering. The group is introduced to three basic approaches to prayer taken from the Christian tradition.

Sharing/Reflecting. In sharing groups, persons discuss which of the three approaches they are most drawn to and why.

Deciding. When the total group assembles, the leader asks the participants to pledge themselves to try one of the approaches to prayer during the coming week. Each person is given the chance to state which approach he or she is choosing and why.

Week Four

Sharing. The class is broken into small groups to discuss how the previous week went. Were they able to pray? What got in the way? If they did pray, what was it like? The total group gathers, and the leader asks for a brief account by three persons of positive experiences of prayer during the past week. The group members then are asked to list the factors that kept them from praying.

Encountering. Passages from Nouwen's *The Genesee Diary* are handed out on a worksheet and then read aloud.[2] These passages describe the various struggles he went through while visiting a Trappist monastery. Prayer is defined not only as something one does in particular times and places but also as an attitude of receptivity to God's will permeating one's entire life.

Reflecting. The group members are asked to reflect on how this view of prayer differs from the one they formed as children and as youth. They are asked to reflect during the coming week on the relationship between prayer as a general attitude and prayer as something done in a specific time and place. They also are asked to continue to pray during the coming week.

Week Five

Reflecting. Each person is given a piece of paper divided into three columns with loneliness, hostility, and illusion at the top of each column. The group is reminded of what Nouwen meant by each of these. Each person is then given time to write down words or phrases in each column that indicate issues he or she is struggling with in each area.

Sharing/Reflecting. In sharing groups, each person shares the one area that he or she would most like to work on through prayer. Through empathetic listening, the sharing groups are asked to reflect back to the person the issues he or she seems to be struggling with in this area. The class is dismissed from the sharing groups.

Week Six

Encountering. The importance of structure and community in sustaining an active prayer life is explored. Practical wisdom from the Christian tradition about such things as regularity of time and place, accountability, and group support are presented. Various books and resources for further reading are presented.

Deciding. Each person is given the chance to design a structure for his or her own time of prayer, including a regular time and place. They are encouraged to anticipate things that might prevent them from praying. At a designated point, cach person finds one other person with whom he or she is comfortable and shares this plan and the potential problems. The leader invites the two people to pray for each other in the coming weeks. The final portion of the class focuses on the possibilities of forming prayer support groups in the future. Different models are described and a sheet circulated to allow people to indicate their interest. The leader accepts responsibility for notifying people with a common interest.

A Weekend Retreat on Spirituality
for Adult Church Members

Friday Evening

Use icebreakers that form people into groups of three or four. They will stay in the same sharing group for the entire weekend.

Remembering. The participants are asked to recollect on paper their experiences of prayer as children and youth.

Sharing. These are shared with the other members of their sharing groups.

Reflection. Each group is asked to come up with its own definition of prayer on the basis of its sharing. This is shared with the entire group.

Break.

Encountering. Passages of Jesus at prayer are studied inductively. The three movements of spirituality found in Henri Nouwen's *Reaching Out* are described: from loneliness to solitude, from hostility to hospitality, and from illusion to prayer.

Saturday Morning

Reflecting. After the group gathers, Nouwen's three movements are written on newsprint. The group is asked: Which of these movements of spirituality did your past prepare you most to undertake? Which least?

Encountering. The group is introduced to three basic approaches to prayer taken from the Christian tradition.

Sharing/Reflecting. In sharing groups, persons discuss which of the three approaches they are most drawn to and why.

Break.

Encountering. After the group reassembles, the leader announces that during the last part of the morning each person will have a chance to try out one of the approaches to prayer. Individuals disperse for time alone.

Saturday Afternoon

Sharing. The group regathers in sharing groups to discuss how the morning prayer time went. Were they able to pray? What got in the way? If they did pray, what was it like? The total group gathers, and the leader asks for a brief account of a positive experience by one member of each sharing group. The group members then are asked to list the factors that made it difficult to pray. Are they likely to encounter the same problems at home?

Encountering. Passages from Nouwen's *The Genesee Diary* are handed out on a worksheet and read aloud. These passages describe the struggles Nouwen went through while visiting a Trappist monastery. Prayer is defined not only as something one does in particular times and places but also as an attitude of receptivity to God's will permeating one's entire life.

Reflecting. The group members are asked to reflect on how this view of prayer differs from the one they formed as children and as youth. They are asked to reflect on the relationship between prayer as an attitude and prayer as something done in a specific time and place.

Afternoon Recreation.

Saturday Evening

Encountering. The group views the movie *Babette's Feast*.

Reflecting. Each person is asked to reflect on a series of questions given to them on a handout. These focus on images of community found in the movie.

Sharing. Each sharing group merges with one other and discusses the movie in light of their reflection. The total group gathers briefly for sharing at the end of the session.

Sunday Morning

Reflecting. Each person is given a piece of paper divided into three columns with loneliness, hostility, and illusion at the top of each column. The group is reminded of what Nouwen meant by each of these. Each person is then given time to write down words or phrases in each column that indicate issues they are struggling with in each area.

Sharing/Reflecting. In sharing groups, each person shares the one area that he or she would most like to work on through prayer. The group is encouraged to listen empathetically and reflect on insights that emerge.

Break.

Encountering. The importance of structure and community to the life of prayer is explored, harking back to *Babette's Feast*. Practical wisdom from the Christian tradition about such things as regularity of time and place, accountability, and group support are presented. Different types of prayer support groups are described, and the total group is encouraged to discuss which models they are most interested in. The ministerial leadership is asked to follow up on this interest.

Deciding. Each person is given the chance to design a structure for his or her own prayer time, including a regular time and place. These are described briefly in sharing groups.

Worship/Deciding. During the worship service, a time of personal testimony is created. Those individuals who wish to are invited to offer what they have learned during the retreat and their renewed commitment to a life of prayer.

Notes

Preface

1. John Calvin, *Institutes of the Christian Religion,* vol. 2, ed. John McNeill, Library of Christian Classics (Philadelphia: Westminster Press, 1960), p. 1018.

2. Karl Barth, *Church Dogmatics,* vol. I.1, eds. G. W. Bromiley and T. Torrance; trans. G. W. Bromiley (Edinburgh: T. & T. Clark, 1975) p. 55.

Chapter 1

1. H. Richard Niebuhr, *Faith on Earth: An Inquiry into the Structure of Human Faith,* ed. Richard R. Niebuhr (New Haven, Conn.: Yale University Press, 1989), p. 12.

Chapter 2

1. See Edward Farley's understanding of theology as a science *and* as a habit in *Theologia: The Fragmentation and Unity of Theological Education* (Philadelphia: Fortress Press, 1983), ch. 2. In my work, I have focused on theology as the reflective dimension of piety. See "Teaching as Practical

Theology" in *Theological Approaches to Christian Education,* eds. J. Seymour and D. Miller (Nashville: Abingdon Press, 1990), ch. 12. See also, *A Teachable Spirit: Recovering the Teaching Office in the Church* (Louisville, Ky.: Westminster/John Knox Press, 1990), pt. 3.

2. I believe the one-on-one emphasis of Roman Catholic spirituality, first fostered in monasticism, is less important in Protestantism than an emphasis on the role of relationships in spiritual formation, especially small group relationships. This is evident in Protestant pietism, the Wesleyan movement, and certain facets of Puritan life.

3. *The Unchurched American: A Gallup Study, 1978* (Princeton, N.J.: The Princeton Religion Research Center, 1978). *The Unchurched American . . . 10 Years Later* (Princeton, N.J.: The Princeton Religion Research Center, 1988).

4. Martin Luther, *The Bondage of the Will,* trans. J. I. Packer and O. R. Johnston (Westwood, N.J.: Fleming H. Revell Co., 1957).

5. Karl Barth suggests this analogy by describing the effect on humanity of God's reconciliation in Christ as a release from prison. See *Church Dogmatics,* vol. IV.1, trans. G. W. Bromiley (Edinburgh: T. & T. Clark, 1956), p. 503.

Chapter 3

1. William Clayton Bower describes the focus of the curriculum he proposes as experienced-based and contrasts it to one that emphasizes bringing "saving truth" to children. See *The Curriculum of Religious Education* (New York: Charles Scribner's Sons, 1927). Similarly, Harrison Elliott writes: "Religious education therefore is not an education with a fixed and predetermined content . . . . Rather, religious education is an enterprise in which historical experiences and conceptions are utilized in a process by which individuals and groups come to experiences and convictions which are mean-

ingful for them today." *Can Religious Education Be Christian?* (New York: Macmillan Co., 1940), p. 310.

2. A good introduction to this is *Cognitive Psychology and Information Processing: An Introduction,* eds. R. Lachman, J. Lachman, and E. Butterfield (Hillsdale, N.J.: Lawrence Erlbaum, 1979).

3. An excellent summary of this research is found in E. D. Hirsch's *Cultural Literacy: What Every American Needs to Know* (New York: Vintage Books, 1987), pp. 33–60. While I have some reservations about Hirsch's constructive proposals, his summary of recent research in cognitive psychology is quite helpful.

4. See especially the models of teaching described under information process in Joyce and Weil's *Models of Teaching,* cited in the Suggested Reading section of this book.

5. See the sermons found in the following: Geoffrey Cuming, *Hippolytus: A Text for Students,* Grove Liturgical Study 8 (Bramcotte Notts, England: Grove Books, 1976); William Telfer, *Cyril of Jerusalem and Nemesis of Emesa,* Library of Christian Classics IV (London: SCM Press, 1955).

6. See T. H. L. Parker's discussion of this in *The Oracles of God: An Introduction to the Preaching of John Calvin* (London: Lutterworth Press, 1945).

7. Wilbert McKeachie, "Improving Lectures by Understanding Students' Information Processing," *New Directions for Teaching and Learning* (San Francisco: Jossey-Bass, 1980), p. 26

8. An excellent discussion of this topic is found in Marie Winn's *The Plug-In Drug* (New York: Bantam Books, 1977).

9. Joseph Lowman, *Mastering the Techniques of Teaching* (San Francisco: Jossey-Bass, 1984), p. 103.

10. McKeachie, "Improving Lectures," p. 30.

11. Ibid., pp. 31–33. See also, Kenneth Eble, *The Craft of Teaching: A Guide to Mastering the Professor's Art* (San Francisco: Jossey-Bass, 1988), pp. 74–77.

12. McKeachie, "Improving Lectures," p. 29.
13. Richard Arends, *Learning to Teach* (New York: Random House, 1988), p. 268.
14. Lowman, *Techniques of Teaching,* p. 108.
15. Louis Rubin, *Artistry in Teaching* (New York: Random House, 1985).
16. Ibid., p. 109.

Chapter 4

1. Peter Benson and Carolyn Eklin, *Effective Christian Education: A National Study of Protestant Congregations—A Summary Report on Faith, Loyalty, and Congregational Life* (Minneapolis: Search Institute 1990).
2. This typology is adapted from Kenneth Moore's *Classroom Teaching Skills: A Primer* (New York: Random House, 1989), pp. 174–78.
3. Richard Arends, *Learning to Teach* (New York: Random House, 1985), p. 289.
4. Moore, *Teaching Skills,* pp. 183–84.
5. Joseph Lowman, *Mastering the Techniques of Teaching* (San Francisco: Jossey-Bass, 1984), p. 136.
6. I have found William Welty's article, "Discussion Method Teaching," to be quite helpful. *Change* 21, no. 4 (July/August 1989): 41–49.
7. Roberta Hestenes has a similar discussion of levels of communication in *Using the Bible in Groups* (Philadelphia: Westminster Press, 1983), pp. 96–97.
8. These are summarized in Ronald Toseland and Robert Rivas' *An Introduction to Group Work Practice* (New York: Macmillan Publishing Co., 1986), pp. 72–75. I have also found Irvin Yalom's characterization of the focal issues of each stage quite helpful. See his *The Theory and Practice of Group Psychotherapy,* 3rd ed. (New York: Basic Books, 1985), chs. 11–12.

Chapter 5

1. George Stroup, *The Promise of Narrative Theology: Recovering the Gospel in the Church* (Atlanta: John Knox Press, 1981); Stanley Hauerwas, *A Community of Character: Toward a Constructive Christian Social Ethic* (Notre Dame, Ind.: University of Notre Dame Press, 1981); Stephen Crites, "The Narrative Quality of Experience," in *Journal of the American Academy of Religion,* 1971, pp. 290–307; Charles Gerkin, *The Living Human Document: Re-visioning Pastoral Counseling in a Hermeneutical Mode* (Nashville: Abingdon Press, 1984).

2. Stroup, cited immediately above, ch. 4. The title of this section was inspired by this chapter.

3. My understanding of this is deeply influenced by H. Richard Niebuhr's description of narrative and revelation in *The Meaning of Revelation* (New York: Macmillan Co., 1941). There he writes on p. 68: "Revelation means for us that part of our inner history which illuminates the rest of it and is itself intelligible."

4. "A Time to Seek," *Newsweek,* December 17, 1990. See also research by the Gallup organization found in *The Unchurched American . . . 10 Years Later* (Princeton, N.J.: The Princeton Religion Research Center, 1988).

5. Augustine, *Confessions,* trans. R. S. Pine-Coffin (Middlesex, England: Penguin Books, 1961), p. 71.

6. Thomas Groome has an excellent discussion of story in this sense. See *Christian Religious Education: Sharing Our Story and Vision* (San Francisco: Harper & Row, 1980), pp. 191–93.

7. This is one of the learning activities used in the Pilgrimage Project mentioned in the Introduction of this book. This can be found in the leader's guide of John and Adrienne Carr's *The Pilgrimage Project: Renewing Our Sense of God's Presence & Purpose—A Group Process,* (Nashville: The Upper Room, 1987) pp. 18–19.

8. This exercise was developed at the Center for Faith Development.

9. See Dietrich Bonhoeffer, *Psalms: The Prayer Book of the Bible,* trans. James Burtness (Minneapolis: Augsburg Publishing House, 1970). Roberta Hestenes has developed an approach that is similar to the one I suggest here. See *Using the Bible in Groups* (Philadelphia: Westminster Press, 1983), pp. 83–84.

10. Irvin Yalom, *The Theory and Practice of Group Psychotherapy,* 3rd ed. (New York: Basic Books, 1985), ch. 2.

11. This exercise was created as part of the Pilgrimage Project, mentioned in n. 7 above.

12. A version of this is found in Carr, *The Pilgrimage Project,* pp. 33–34.

13. Stroup, *The Promise of Narrative Theology,* p. 171.

14. The crisis paradigm that is implied in the "collision" metaphor points to a total discontinuity between the processes of identity formation and ongoing human transformation. The Christian life, however, is not a series of discrete collisions with the Word of God, but involves an unfolding dialectic of identity formation (by which identity narratives providing continuity are shaped within communities of faith) and ongoing transformation which reorients these narratives.

15. See Roberta Hestenes' discussion of this learning activity in *Using the Bible in Groups,* pp. 78–79.

16. This learning activity emerged during my work on the Pilgrimage Project, mentioned above, but was not written up in the Carrs' material.

17. Sidney Jourard, *The Transparent Self* (New York: Van Nostrand Reinhold Co., 1971), p. 13.

18. This learning activity is described in Sara Little's *Learning Together in the Christian Fellowship* (Richmond: John Knox Press, 1956), pp. 49–50 and Martha Leypoldt's *40 Ways to Teach in Groups* (Valley Forge, Pa.: Judson Press, 1967), pp. 49–50.

19. Carr, *The Pilgrimage Project,* pp. 51–53.

Chapter 6

1. As the Athanasian Creed puts it: "The Father incomprehensible, the Son incomprehensible, and the Holy Ghost incomprehensible." Quoted in John Macquarrie's *Principles of Christian Theology,* 2nd ed. (New York: Charles Scribner's Sons, 1966), p. 203.

2. See Tom Long's discussion of this in *Preaching and the Literary Forms of the Bible,* (Philadelphia: Fortress Press, 1989), p. 88.

3. Long, cited immediately above, notes that the term *parable* is used to cover a wide range of literary forms and is difficult to pin down. I am drawing on the work of John Crossan and Sallie McFague, among others, to provide a definition that focuses on the element of reversal. John Dominic Crossan, *Raid on the Articulate: Cosmic Eschatology in Jesus and Borges* (New York: Harper & Row, 1976); *Parables* (New York: Harper & Row, 1973). Sallie McFague, *Speaking in Parables: A Study in Metaphor and Theology* (Philadelphia: Fortress Press, 1975).

4. Crossan, *Raid on the Articulate,* p. 41.

5. John Crossan has emphasized this especially. Crossan's book, *Raid on the Articulate,* has already been mentioned. See pp. 98ff. See also his article, "Paradox Gives Rise to Metaphor: Paul Ricoeur's Hermeneutics and the Parables of Jesus" in *Biblical Research* (Chicago Society of Biblical Research, 1979–80). In the former, he describes parable as a paradox formed into story, affecting a structural reversal on a traditional or expected story.

6. *The Compact Edition of the Oxford English Dictionary,* vol. 2/P–Z (London: Oxford University Press, 1971), p. 450. Watzlawick, Beavin, and Jackson describe three kinds of paradoxes: (1) logico-mathematical paradoxes (antinomies), (2) paradoxical definitions (semantic antinomies), and (3) pragmatic paradoxes. *Pragmatics of Human Communication: A Study of Interactional Patterns, Pathologies, and Paradoxes*

(New York: W. W. Norton & Co., 1967), ch. 6. Our interest primarily is in the third type.

7. *The Encyclopedia of Philosophy*, vol. 5, Paul Edwards, ed. (New York: Macmillan Co., 1967), p. 45.

8. The term "frame of reference" will be described more fully at a later point in this chapter. It draws heavily on cognitive psychology and communication theory approaches to human behavior.

9. See Peter Elbow, *Embracing Contraries: Explorations in Learning and Teaching* (New York: Oxford University Press, 1986). Kieran Egan, *Educational Development* (New York: Oxford University Press, 1979), especially ch. 4 and pp. 133–35. Excellent examples of paradoxical thinking are found in the parables of Kierkegaard. See *Parables of Kierkegaard*, ed. Thomas Oden (Princeton, N.J.: Princeton University Press, 1978).

10. This example is developed artfully in William Placher's *Unapologetic Theology: A Christian Voice in a Pluralistic Conversation* (Louisville, Ky.: Westminster/John Knox Press, 1989), p. 124.

11. This problem is found in a number of places. See Paul Watzlawick, John Weakland, and Richard Fisch, *Change: Principle of Problem Formation and Problem Resolution* (New York: W. W. Norton & Co., 1974), p. 25.

12. James Loder describes the "grammar" of transformation in his book, *The Transforming Moment: Understanding Convictional Experiences* (San Francisco: Harper & Row, 1981). See especially, ch. 2. I am focusing primarily on only one moment in the process of transformation as Loder describes it. For a more comprehensive use of Loder's work, see Margaret Krych's book, *Teaching the Gospel Today: A Guide for Education in the Congregation* (Minneapolis: Augsburg Publishing House, 1987).

13. Watzlawick, Weakland, and Fisch, *Change*, pp. 94–95.

14. Research on the intellectual and moral development of college students seems to reveal something along these lines.

The work of William Perry, Lawrence Kohlberg, and Carol Gilligan reveals a "relativistic" phase in many college students upon their exposure to values, beliefs, and lifestyles different from the ones with which they were raised. This relativism represents the students' initial response to pluralism and an awareness of the limits of every frame of reference. Typically, this phase is surpassed by one in which the relative adequacy of some perspectives over others is acknowledged, while a recognition of the limits of every perspective is maintained. Perry, *Forms of Intellectual and Ethical Development in the College Years: A Scheme* (New York: Holt, Rinehart & Winston, 1968). Kohlberg and Gilligan, "The Adolescent as a Philosopher: The Discovery of the Self in a Postconventional World," *Daedalus* 100 (1971): 1072.

15. The differences between these two schools is more complex than this, to be sure. The New School position contained a number of persons who were not primarily revivalistic in their orientation. See Lefferts Loetscher's discussion of this in *A Brief History of the Presbyterians*, 4th ed. (Philadelphia: Westminster Press, 1978), pp. 96ff. This could be easily pointed out in teaching, while maintaining the basic contrast.

16. The concept of anomalies has received a great deal of attention in recent years in the philosophy of science. Thomas Kuhn in particular has called attention to the fact that all scientific research has some anomalies. He argues that there is always some data or evidence that cannot be explained by a scientific theory. See *The Structure of Scientific Revolutions*, 2nd ed. (Chicago: University of Chicago Press, 1962).

Appendix

1. Henri Nouwen, *Reaching Out: The Three Movements of the Spiritual Life* (Garden City, N.Y.: Doubleday & Co., 1975).

2. Henri Nouwen, *The Genesee Diary: Report from a Trappist Monastery* (Garden City, N.Y.: Doubleday & Co., 1976).

Suggested Reading

Books Suggesting a Variety
of Practical Teaching Methods

Griggs, Donald. *Basic Skills for Church Teachers.* Nashville: Abingdon Press, 1985.

————*Planning for Teaching Church School.* Valley Forge, Pa.: Judson Press, 1985.

————*Teaching Teachers to Teach.* Livermore, Calif.: Griggs Educational Service, 1974. These three books by Griggs provide excellent ideas on how to teach and give many practical suggestions. Good place to start. .

Layman, James. *Using Case Studies in Church Education.* Scottsdale, Ariz.: National Teacher Education Project, 1977. One of the few good books for teachers that gives practical help on how to use case studies in the classroom. Gives suggestions about finding good cases and writing your own.

LeFever, Marlene. *Creative Teaching Methods.* Elgin, Ill.: David C. Cook, 1985. Covers a wide range of teaching approaches, including drama, role-play, simulation games, discussion, and others. Quite practical and useful. Dares you to be creative!

Swift, Helen, and Frank Oppenheim. *The Mustard Seed Process: Twelve Practical Exercises on Social Justice for Groups and Individuals.* Mahwah, N.J.: Paulist Press, 1986. Short scenarios that are helpful discussion starters. Provides good questions to get the conversation going.

Books Dealing with the Five Aspects of Teaching Commitment

1. *Remembering*

Baddeley, Alan. *Your Memory: A User's Guide—How Our Minds Store, Retrieve and Use Information.* New York: Macmillan Publishing Co., 1982. Does not focus directly on teaching, but provides a readable introduction to recent research on human memory. Includes chapters on learning and improving memory.

Carr, John, and Adrienne Carr, *The Pilgrimage Project: Renewing Our Sense of God's Presence and Purpose.* Nashville: The Upper Room, 1987. Includes a leader's guide and participant's book. Offers a series of learning activities that cover almost all the teaching aspects. Designed for small group sharing in a retreat or series. Many wonderful exercises for remembering as well as for the four other aspects.

Keck, L. Robert. *The Spirit of Synergy: God's Power and You.* Nashville: Abingdon Press, 1978. Poor theology but excellent examples of meditative prayers. Gives insight into writing and using guided imagery in remembering.

Klug, Ron. *How to Keep a Spiritual Journal.* Nashville: Thomas Nelson Publishers, 1982. Easy-to-use guide on how to write a journal for remembering and reflecting. Good bibliography and list of published journals by famous persons.

Progoff, Ira. *At a Journal Workshop: The Basic Text and Guide for Using the Intensive Journal.* New York: Dialogue House Library, 1975. *The* book on journaling. Quite involved and works best if you have attended a workshop teaching you how to use it. Covers remembering and reflecting.

Williams, Linda Verlee. *Teaching for the Two-Sided Mind: A Guide to Right Brain/Left Brain Education.* New York: Simon & Schuster, 1983. Discusses recent research on the brain and offers helpful suggestions on how teachers can address both the rational and creative sides of the brain. Helpful for focused and meditative remembering.

2. *Reflecting*

Larson, Roland, and Doris Larson, *Values and Faith: Value-Clarifying Exercises for Family and Church Groups.* Minneapolis: Winston Press, 1976. A helpful collection of values clarification exercises that are adapted to issues of importance to the church.

Simon, Sidney, Leland How, and Howard Kirschenbaum. *Values Clarification: A Handbook of Practical Strategies for Teachers and Students.* New York: Hart Publishing Co., 1972. Not specifically religious but provides a number of practical exercises that can help people reflect upon their experiences and clarify their values.

Simon, Sidney. *Meeting Yourself Halfway: 31 Value Clarification Strategies for Daily Living.* Niles, Ill.: Argus Communications, 1974. Provides a number of enjoyable exercises for reflection by individuals. Can be used in groups as well.

Williams, Susan. *What Do You Think: Teaching Critical Thinking on Critical Issues.* St. Louis: Institute for Peace and Justice, 1987. Short but excellent guide to the issue of critical thinking. Suggests a variety of methods to foster critical thinking.

3. *Encounter*

Brown, Robert McAfee. *Unexpected News: Reading the Bible with Third World Eyes.* Philadelphia: Westminster

Press, 1984. Written from a liberation theology perspective. Helps an individual or group view the Bible through the eyes of the third world. Clear and well-written.

Coleman, Lyman, Denny Rydberg, Richard Peace, and Gary Christopherson, eds. *Serendipity New Testament for Groups.* Mahwah, N.J.: Paulist Press, 1986. Provides questions for reflection and further research on the entire New Testament.

Griggs, Donald. *Translating the Good News through Teaching Activities.* Nashville: Abingdon Press, 1973. Provides many helpful, practical teaching activities that can be used to teach the Bible to all ages.

Hestenes, Roberta. *Using the Bible in Groups.* Philadelphia: Westminster Press, 1983. A gold mine of practical strategies for teaching the Bible. Includes excellent introduction on how to set up a small group and various stages of group life.

Maas, Robin. *Church Bible Study Handbook.* Nashville: Abingdon Press, 1982. Extremely helpful overview of all aspects of Bible study. Combines a scholarly interest in the use of modern research without sacrificing practical concerns.

Martin, George. *Reading Scripture as the Word of God: Practical Approaches and Attitudes,* 2nd ed. Ann Arbor, Mich.: Servant Books, 1975. Valuable introduction to the study of scripture in the context of a devotional life. Clear, well-written, accessible.

Ramsay, DeVere. *Glimpses of the Gospel Through Art: Intergenerational Bible Studies.* Durham, N.C.: National Teacher Education Program, 1990. Students reflect on their own art in relation to Christian art. Includes prints of famous works of Christian art from many periods. A good way to creatively encounter the history of the church and its different understandings of Jesus.

Smart, James. *The Strange Silence of the Bible in the Church: A Study of Hermeneutics.* Philadelphia: Westminster

Press, 1970. An excellent introduction to important issues involved in the interpretation of scripture. Not overly technical but requires serious study.

Smith, Judy Gattis. *Teaching to Wonder: Spiritual Growth through Imagination and Movement.* Nashville: Parthenon Press, 1989. An excellent introduction to the use of the imagination in teaching. Concrete help in allowing our students to encounter God through scripture at the level of the image and story.

Wink, Walter. *Transforming Bible Study.* Nashville: Abingdon Press, 1980. Introduction to a highly creative way of engaging scripture. Fosters imagination and feeling.

4. Sharing

Griffin, Em. *Getting Together: A Guide for Good Groups* Downers Grove, Ill.: Inter-Varsity Press, 1982. Clear, humorous overview of groups. Great cartoon illustrations.

Hill, Dorothy LaCroix. *Leading a Group: A Guide to Your Preparation.* Nashville: Discipleship Resources, United Methodist Church, 1966. Older book but still a valuable introduction to basic issues in leading a group.

Johnson, David, and Frank Johnson. *Joining Together: Group Theory and Group Skills,* 2nd ed. Englewood Cliffs, N.J.: Prentice-Hall, 1982. Introduction to theory and practice of groups. Covers many aspects of group life, from leadership to conflict.

Johnson, David, Roger Johnson, Edythe Holubec, and Patricia Roy. *Circles of Learning: Cooperation in the Classroom.* Alexandria, Va.: Association for Supervision and Curriculum Development, 1984. An excellent introduction to the concept of cooperative learning. Explores the importance of people learning together and the dangers of structuring all learning in a competitive fashion.

Leypoldt, Martha. *Forty Ways to Teach in Groups.* Valley Forge, Pa.: Judson Press, 1967. Offers forty practical methods for teaching groups that are useful in many situations. A good place to get new ideas.

Little, Sara. *Learning Together in the Christian Fellowship.* Richmond: John Knox Press, 1956. Reprinted many times and generally considered a classic. Provides many ideas on how to teach in group settings. Practical and theological. The best place to start.

5. *Deciding*

Leypoldt, Martha. *Learning Is Change: Adult Education in the Church.* Valley Forge, Pa.: Judson Press, 1971. Offers a host of practical exercises useful in many teaching situations. Describes a broad process of change of which decision is one part.

Purdy, John. *Returning God's Call: The Challenge of Christian Living.* Louisville: Westminster/John Knox Press, 1989. Explores various aspects of the Christian's calling as found in the Bible. Challenges contemporary Christians to live out their calling in today's world.

Basic Texts on Teaching

Bowman, Locke. *Teaching Today: The Church's First Ministry.* Philadelphia: Westminster Press, 1980. Good overview of church's teaching ministry in the context of its entire ministry.

Brueggemann, Walter. *The Creative Word: Canon as a Model for Biblical Education.* Philadelphia: Fortress Press, 1982. Written by a scholar of the Bible. The canon of scripture seen as providing basic models for the teaching task. Provocative.

Cully, Iris, and Kendig Cully, eds. *Harper's Encyclopedia of Religious Education.* San Francisco: Harper & Row, 1990. Introduction to basic concepts of teaching and education, especially as they relate to church.

Foster, Charles. *Teaching in the Community of Faith.* Nashville: Abingdon Press, 1982. Excellent discussion of the nature of teaching in the church. Chapter 4 is a goldmine.

Groome, Thomas. *Christian Religious Education: Sharing Our Story and Vision.* San Francisco: Harper & Row, 1980. One of the most influential books written in recent years. Develops a "Shared Praxis" approach to teaching that is deep but usable.

Harris, Maria. *Teaching and Religious Imagination: An Essay in the Theology of Teaching.* San Francisco: Harper & Row, 1987. Highly creative book by a highly creative teacher. Will challenge you to be more imaginative in your teaching.

Hyman, Ronald. *Ways of Teaching,* 2nd ed. Philadelphia: J. B. Lippincott Co., 1974. Demanding but rewarding text for serious readers. Covers many teaching methods, from discussion to sociodrama.

Joyce, Bruce, and Marsha Weil, *Models of Teaching,* 3rd ed. Englewood Cliffs, N.J.: Prentice-Hall, 1972. Introduction to different approaches to teaching, based on various theories in the field. *The* standard introduction.

Krych, Margaret. *Teaching the Gospel Today: A Guide for Education in the Congregation.* Minneapolis: Augsburg Publishing House, 1987. Theologically informed. Draws on James Loder's understanding of human transformation to form a new theory of teaching.

Landau, Elliott, Sherrie Epstein, and Ann Stone, eds. *The Teaching Experience: An Introduction to Education through Literature.* Englewood Cliffs, N.J.: Prentice-Hall, 1976. Wonderful collection of literature focusing on the teacher.

Little, Sara. *To Set One's Heart: Belief and Teaching in the Church.* Atlanta: John Knox Press, 1983. Best place to start for an overview of teaching models. Describes five basic approaches to teaching and their relevance to belief-formation in the church.

McCollough, Charles. *Heads of Heaven, Feet of Clay: Ideas and Stories for Adult Education*. New York: Pilgrim Press, 1983. A helpful, readable overview of significant trends in recent Christian education. Provides practical guidelines for how to create education designs on the basis of theory.

Merriam, Sharan, ed., *Themes of Adulthood through Literature*. New York: Teachers College Press, 1983. Snippets of literature describing human development at various points. Very useful in teaching.

Osmer, Richard Robert. *A Teachable Spirit: Recovering the Teaching Office in the Church*. Louisville: Westminster/ John Knox Press, 1990. An examination of the crisis of the teaching ministry in mainline Protestantism. Attempts to recover classic understandings of the teaching office as found in Luther and Calvin.

Palmer, Parker. *To Know as We Are Known: A Spirituality of Education*. San Francisco: Harper & Row, 1983. Criticizes tendency of education to treat truth as an object. Invites learners and teachers to form a living relationship with truth.

Smart, James. *The Teaching Ministry of the Church: An Examination of the Basic Principles of Christian Education*. Philadelphia: Westminster Press, 1954. Classic statement of the church's teaching ministry from the perspective of Karl Barth's theology. Old but still unique in its perspective.